My Father
AND
Atticus Finch

My Father
AND
Atticus Finch

A LAWYER'S FIGHT FOR
JUSTICE IN 1930s ALABAMA

Joseph Madison Beck

THE UNIVERSITY OF GEORGIA PRESS
ATHENS

Paperback edition published in 2018
by the University of Georgia Press
Athens, Georgia 30602
www.ugapress.org
© 2016 by Joseph Madison Beck
All rights reserved
Book design by Fearn de Vicq

Most University of Georgia Press titles are
available from popular e-book vendors.

Printed digitally

Library of Congress Cataloging-in-Publication Data

Names: Beck, Joseph Madison, author.
Title: My father and Atticus Finch : a lawyer's fight for justice in 1930s
Alabama / By Joseph Madison Beck.
Description: Athens, Georgia : The University of Georgia Press, 2018.
Identifiers: LCCN 2017053875 | ISBN 9780820353081 (pbk. : alk. paper)
Subjects: LCSH: Beck, Foster (Lawyer) | Criminal defense
lawyers—Alabama—Biography. | Defense (Criminal procedure)—Alabama. |
Trials (Rape)—Alabama—History. | Race relations—Alabama—History.
Classification: LCC KF373.B3495 B43 2018 | DDC 345.761/02532—dc23
LC record available at https://lccn.loc.gov/2017053875

For Kay,
Theo, and
Anna

Preface

MY FATHER did not "sell for his worth." His sister told me that and my mother did not disagree. What did that mean, I wondered as a child. Only as an adult did I trace it to a time before my birth when, as a young white lawyer, he represented a black man charged with raping a white woman in a small town in south Alabama. My interest intensified as time went on because this was my father; because, like him, I became a lawyer; and because people kept saying his case could have inspired Harper Lee's celebrated novel, *To Kill a Mockingbird*.

For a while, the thought that the defendant's lawyer in *Mockingbird* could have been modeled on Foster Campbell Beck—my father!—was enough for me. When even Ms. Lee, in a gracious letter forwarded to me by her agent, acknowledged the "obvious parallels" (adding that she could not "recall" my father's case and that her work was "fiction"), I decided it was time to find out more for myself.

MY MANUSCRIPT was accepted for publication prior to the release of Ms. Lee's *Go Set a Watchman*, a book that brings to mind the question: who is the real Atticus Finch—the beloved lawyer in *Mockingbird* or the paternalistic bigot of *Watchman*? The truth is, there were both kinds of Atticus—and many variations of them—in south Alabama in those days.

Some have insisted that the Atticus of *Mockingbird* was an idealized Southern white man who never existed, and that the racist Atticus of *Watchman* is the accurate portrayal. But that is not the whole truth. My father never subscribed to racist reading materials and never attended a meeting of the White Citizens' Council or the Klan; he despised both organizations. I never heard him refer to Negroes (as African Americans were properly called when I was growing up) as "backward" or "in their childhood as a people," or say anything at all like that. On the other hand, like the Atticus of *Mockingbird*, my father forbade use of the word "nigger," accepted farm produce from indigent clients in payment for legal work, and, most importantly, courageously defended a black man wrongfully accused in 1930s' Alabama of raping a white woman.

If you miss the Atticus of *Mockingbird*, if you feel sad about the Atticus of *Watchman*, keep reading. This book is about neither of those fictional characters; instead, it is about a real life lived with conviction.

WHAT FOLLOWS is based not only on conversations with my parents but also on my father's handwritten family history, newspaper articles about that case, the transcript of the trial, and the Alabama Supreme Court opinion; all of that is factual. As I was not born until five years after the trial, sometimes I must surmise, from knowledge of my family and the times, what may have been said, what surely was said. I believe that content to be factual as well, even though the words have not previously been set down on paper.

Foster Beck was dying when he began work on our family history, and he had just begun describing the case when his handwriting stops in the middle of this sentence: "[The prosecution] . . . produced testimony that the defendant was purported to be a . . ."

Fortunately, I remember him telling me a lot more about *State of Alabama v. Charles White, Alias,* starting with how the case came to him.

My Father
AND
Atticus Finch

Chapter 1

JUDGE W. L. PARKS began the telephone call to Foster Beck with the customary courtesies, asking first after his father, then about his law practice. Other questions too: about the dry spell, fishing conditions. Finally, in his own good time, the judge said what he was calling about, the rape case there in Troy.

It was news to Foster, who had not heard about a rape in Troy. Troy was thirty-seven miles away. Foster cleared his throat. "A rape case, Judge?" In the same moment, he heard a familiar click. "Talking with the court, if you please, ma'am." He was hoping the elderly lady he shared a party line with would stop listening in.

Negro from up North, Judge Parks said. Goes by Charles White, but he's had some aliases. And it was a rape of a white girl. The judge seemed surprised Foster didn't know. It was all over the Troy and Montgomery papers.

Foster was straining to hear. Outside, a pair of mules had run a wagon into a gully that had washed out back in April. The Negro driver and two other Negro workers from a local peanut farm were loudly arguing over what to do about the broken axle. With the judge's permission, Foster set down the telephone receiver and went to close the window. Then he returned to the rolltop desk his father had loaned him and picked up the telephone receiver and slid the electric fan closer to his chair.

The Troy bar, Judge Parks was saying, the ones who could try a case, got themselves appointed special prosecutors.

Foster knew why the Troy lawyers did that—to create a conflict of interest so they wouldn't have to take the case. He felt a twitch in his stomach.

The judge teased Foster a little, about not smiling much. Then he said he'd heard about the bastardy case Foster had brought against the son of a prominent man there in Enterprise.

"The boy made that girl pregnant, Judge. There wasn't really much of a dispute to it once the boy's father admitted on the stand the child was his spitting image." Even with the closed window, Foster could hear a white man outside his office berating the Negro driver for letting the mules run the wagon into the gully.

All the same, Judge Parks was impressed. It took guts, he said, to bring a bastardy claim in Enterprise against that boy. That family. For bastardy! The judge's voice was laced with merriment and his tone invited Foster to respond in kind.

Foster had been told for years that he did not smile enough and he had tried to work on it, but he did not laugh or even smile when he replied, "I won for her the princely sum of one hundred dollars per year, Judge, that's all there was to it." He was becoming uncomfortable about where this was heading.

Judge Parks said he knew the statute, knew a hundred dollars a year was all the law gave. And then he said he wanted Foster to be the lawyer for Charles White, Alias. That was all there was to it.

I HAVE NO DOUBT that the much publicized, so-called Scottsboro decisions a few years earlier by the United States Supreme Court were on the mind of Judge Parks. I know they were on the mind of my father who told me years later of his disgust and embarrassment that his beloved Alabama had denied simple justice to nine black male teenagers accused of raping two white girls. The first convictions had been reversed because the Alabama trial judge had refused to allow time for the defense lawyers to prepare, resulting in a denial of due process of law; the second convictions—this time the defense lawyer was the brilliant and esteemed Samuel Leibowitz of New York—were also reversed because black citizens had been systematically excluded from being called for possible jury duty.

"I have a pretty full calendar right now, Judge," Foster stalled. The fact was, he had very little on his calendar and needed work. His reputation was growing but his savings were shrinking. He had stopped several farm foreclosures since the first of the year, receiving two sides of salt pork, a dozen jars of blackberry jam, and a cord of firewood in payment. And he had gotten an unwed mother one hundred dollars and the public judgment of Enterprise that even the powerful had to stand before the law. Government of laws, not of men; he was proud of that. People in Enterprise seemed to like his results, too. But defending a Negro for raping a white woman? He needed time to think.

Judge Parks was determined. He could work with Foster's calendar. Besides, there was not going to be a trial. The Negro had already confessed. But the judge still wanted him to have first-class representation for the sentencing by a son of Alabama. If Foster didn't take the case, and with all the Troy lawyers having a "conflict," Roosevelt would send some Jew lawyer from New York.

My father told me that he had to smile just a little when the judge said that. He was pretty sure Judge Parks didn't know any Jewish lawyers from New York. My father knew some, though, because he had gone to the University of Alabama with them. He had not been afraid of them. The truth was, the Jewish law students from New York were the ones who had been afraid, but they came anyway, all the way to Tuscaloosa, for the best education they could afford; and he told me it had given him pride that they thought the University of Alabama was a good place to study law, with all the schools up in New York.

"Judge, let me think about it. I'll tell you something next week."

Judge Parks's tone turned impatient. "You know I can appoint you," he said. It was a statement, not a question.

Foster was not sure that was true; he was from neighboring Coffee County, not Pike County where the trial would be held, although both counties were in the same circuit. But he was curious and he couldn't help but be flattered that he was being asked to take the case, so he said, "When'd this happen?"

Judge Parks was incredulous. It happened Tuesday. Didn't Foster get the *Messenger*? The better class in Enterprise took the *Troy Messenger* as well as the *Enterprise Ledger*. Foster took the *Messenger* and the *Ledger*. He also took the *Atlanta Constitution*.

"*Messenger* gets here a day late." Foster saw yesterday's unread stack of papers where the maid had left them. He couldn't throw away a newspaper until he'd read it. In that way, he was like his father, who read a dozen papers a week, from Troy, Montgomery, Atlanta, Chicago, New York, all over.

Judge Parks told Foster to read the front page of the Tuesday paper. Judge Parks said he had asked the reporter to withhold his name, but that he was the one who had ordered Charles White to be rushed from the Troy jail to Kilby prison in Montgomery. The judge didn't want a lynching there in Troy. It was 1938, not '28. The judge cleared his throat. He told Foster again that he wanted him to do it. Then he said, "Foster, your daddy would want you to do it."

Chapter 2

THANKFULLY, I don't have to rely only on my father's handwritten history for an image of the man Judge Parks called "your daddy." That man was my grandfather, whom I was told to address as Granddaddy.

I saw him often. More than half a century later, I can still see his gangly frame, the dark, melancholy eyes, the squared-off, weathered face and uncombed iron-gray hair, the gold watch chain hanging across his belly. And there were his smells—of tobacco and of something else that I was not able to identify at the time, bourbon; only in later years did I learn about his borderline alcoholism, much later about his use of cocaine. He and I were the best of friends until his death when I was twelve years old, although I suspect that he liked me mostly because I was the only male heir to carry forward the name Madison Beck, a suspicion partially confirmed in a strange, rambling letter about "a lonely old man," written to me the year I was born but ceremoniously withheld until my tenth birthday, and signed "Granddaddy for whom you are named."

My father would have bridled when Judge Parks brought up his

father, calling him "your daddy" instead of calling him "Mr. M. L."
Everyone who wasn't blood kin called Madison Lewis Beck "Mr.
M. L." Sometimes my father even referred to him that way outside
the family. But what he would have resented more was Judge Parks's
presumption: that because of his father's reputation as a progressive
on race, he should take the case.

Mr. M. L.'s reputation was not altogether justified, just comparatively so. He had cordial relations with "the colored." There was a
chair reserved for him at a favorite black church where he went on
occasion—sometimes to their funerals, sometimes just to hear, as
he put it, "singing as only Negroes sing." The Negro women especially loved him, and for good reason. Their men could take their
pay at the M. L. Beck sawmill in special M. L. Beck coins or in the
regular Yankee dollars—their choice. The women pushed for taking
the M. L. Becks because they were only good at M. L. Beck General Merchandise, which had never sold the men alcohol, not before,
during, or after Prohibition. I still have an M. L. Beck coin, "Good
for 25 cents merchandise."

My father wrote in the family history that his father paid his
black workers "above the usual wage for the community" and that,
unlike some white employers, he "tried to not let them get in debt
to him. . . . Nevertheless, these blacks were expected to come in
the back door and sit in the kitchen when they came to the house."
Thus, while he believed his mother and father were "quite tolerant"
by the standards of the time, he added, "I would [also] say that they
were paternalistic."

Paternalism alone did not make Mr. M. L. a progressive on race.
And although it was pretty well known in parts of south Alabama
that Mr. M. L. and the Jacksons and Joe Cassady had driven the

Klan out of Crenshaw County in 1935, and that they did it partly to protect the county's black population, even that didn't make Mr. M. L. a progressive on race in the minds of the better class of whites, who thought that however much good the Klan had done during Reconstruction, by the 1930s they were just troublemakers.

The idea that Mr. M. L. was not just paternalistic but progressive probably got started with the controversy over Will Pickett, a dark, smooth-skinned black man who was in debt to a rival sawmill owner. Mr. M. L. paid off Will's debt so that he wouldn't be arrested and hired him to work in his own sawmill. "I don't hold with peonage," he said when the rival called him a nigger lover while the two were standing toe to toe, fists balled, at the flowing well in Glenwood. The story was told and retold in Glenwood, Mr. M. L.'s commercial base in Crenshaw County, and repeated as far as Troy and Enterprise. Most in south Alabama saw it as only partly about being a racial progressive, and at least as much about Mr. M. L. outsmarting a competitor and gaining a dependable employee (except on Saturday night when, according to the family history, Will would drink, stagger to town, get arrested for sassing some white person and wind up in Glenwood's small jail until Monday morning, when my grandfather would pay his seven-dollar fine and send him to the mill with a big headache and a reprimand).

It was my grandfather's relationship with Tump Garner—a remarkable black man I had the honor of knowing myself when I was a boy—more than buying Will Pickett out of peonage, that got the idea started that Mr. M. L. really *was* a progressive on race. According to our family history, Tump could saw an order of lumber, repair a steam engine, and grind meal to fool the folks who thought water-ground meal was the only meal fit to eat. He could take a log hook and turn the log before the average man, white or black, could get his hook set. On Emancipation Day, Tump celebrated by leading the Glenwood Negroes against the Goshen Negroes in baseball, playing any position with or without a glove, all the while chanting and singing as the whites sat on the side cheering and passing the hat when he hit a home run. By the time my father went off to college, Tump was Mr. M. L.'s sawyer, millwright, and miller. When the family's Model T, the first in Glenwood, broke down, Tump, who had never before even seen a car, took it apart and fixed it so that—as Mr. M. L. swore to one and all—it ran better than when it was new. All of which made it only fair, Mr. M. L. reasoned, that Tump should be paid better than the whites he courteously supervised at the sawmill, even if that led some in Glenwood to grumble that Mr. M. L. was turning a little *too* progressive on race.

My father told me that his father also had his blind spots. There was the time, again reported in the family history, when my father prepared a letter to a Negro who owed Mr. M. L. money on an account. My father began the letter with the customary salutation, "Dear Sir." Mr. M. L. had him rewrite the letter, suggesting he leave off the "Dear Sir" and just write the one word, "Tom," as the salutation.

Progressive or not, my grandfather discussed race with my father infrequently. One occasion I heard about was when Mr. M. L. had been drinking in the afternoon. "You free a million illiterate slaves, I'm fine with that," he said. "Slavery never was right. But, after the War, you had Nigras getting the vote before they tried on their first pair of shoes. Measures had to be taken. I was too young to understand it all, but I do believe the Jim Crow laws were meant to be temporary. Granted, over the years, those laws became a way of life, and these days, we're stuck with 'em."

My grandfather, like a lot of Southerners, sometimes said "Nigra" instead of "Negro," but he fiercely insisted, to my father and to anyone who challenged him, that saying "Nigra" was not the same as saying "nigger," that "Nigra" was exactly the same as saying "Negro" only with a Southern accent. My father remembered getting his mouth washed out with soap for saying the word "nigger" and the word "fuck" when he was six years old, just repeating what other boys said at school—washed out once for each bad word.

Chapter 3

"**I**F I TAKE this case, Judge," Foster said, "I will just do it on my own, sir." He was trying not to sound defensive or disrespectful. "Don't bring Daddy into it, please, sir."

Judge Parks tut-tutted but did not apologize.

"It's all right, Judge, but I want to think about it. And I want to meet my client while I'm thinking about it. My possible client. Can you get me in to see him?"

Judge Parks could do that. He would call the warden at Kilby himself. Driving to Montgomery, Foster would go right through Troy, so he should stop on the way back and they would see what was what.

When Foster did not respond, the judge reminded him about the article in the *Messenger*. If Foster couldn't find it, the judge would clip it and give him his own copy. It would tell him all he needed to know.

The June 8, 1938, *Messenger* was there in his office, at the bottom of the stack, under the Atlanta paper of the day before. The article about Charles White was on page one, under the headline "NEGRO RUSHED TO KILBY PRISON AFTER ATTACK."

"A wandering negro fortune teller, giving the name of C. W. White," the *Messenger* reported, was removed from the Troy jail "for safekeeping" following his attack on a local white girl. The *Messenger* explained that the white girl had been "enticed" to the site of the crime by "a negro woman, Mary Etta Bray," for the purpose of having her fortune told. As word of the crime was passed and with feelings running "high," the attacker's female accomplice was also delivered to Montgomery for safekeeping.

At Kilby, the *Messenger* reported, "the negro volunteered a detailed confession of the attack" and the confession was reduced to writing and signed in the presence of numerous law enforcement officials.

A physician, called to attend to the girl, later confirmed that "the negro had accomplished his dastardly purpose."

Foster clipped the article from the *Messenger* with scissors and slipped it into an empty cubbyhole in the rolltop desk. He wanted to think about what he had read. First of all, there was a confession. That meant the only thing he could do would be to get Charles White a term of years instead of the electric chair. That should be easy: the state of Alabama could not ask for the death penalty if it had obtained the confession in return for a promise of a life sentence. He could drive to Montgomery to meet White, stop over in Troy to negotiate the plea, and be back the same day, depending on the weather and the roads, and then he'd be done with it. Most people in Enterprise—unless someone had listened in on the party line to his conversation with Judge Parks—would never learn of the case, and if some found out, the better class of people, the ones who could pay cash money for his work, would see it for what it was. After the Scottsboro cases, it became law that Alabama must provide a Negro with a lawyer in all future capital cases. Surely, the better class knew that much from all the talk about Scottsboro—they might even quietly thank him for handling the matter rather than having someone come down to Troy from the North and act superior.

Practicalities aside, he was still in his thirties, still idealistic, reverent about the Constitution—a government of laws, not of men—and not yet immune to the siren call, the image of himself as the lone lawyer standing for the unpopular client because it was right that a man have a lawyer. It was why, really, he went to law school to begin with. He had liked himself when defending farmers and sharecroppers, white and colored, from the banks, and never mind that most of his clients couldn't pay cash money—he was getting by all right, and with each win for the poor, the commercial interests of Enterprise and all of Coffee County were taking note that he could win hard cases. With their growing respect would eventually come more paying work; it was just a matter of time.

Beginning to feel better about the Charles White matter, Foster leaned back in his office chair and turned to his right, so that the electric fan could cool the left side of his face, and stared out the office window he had reopened after all the shouting over the broken wagon axle subsided. The magnolia blossoms across the street, in front of the funeral home, were creamy white perfections, proof to him that if there were a God, he was a master artist.

If I leave early in the morning, he thought, I can be at Kilby prison before noon, assuming the roads to Montgomery are dry, see about this Charles White, Alias, and be back in Enterprise the same afternoon.

Chapter 4

MY FATHER WAS RAISED by parents who were fairly well educated for post-Civil War Alabama. "My mother and father," he wrote, "both attended the Male and Female Institute at Highland Home, Alabama, about 30 miles away [from Glenwood]. They boarded there during the school term and, for the times, it was considered to be an outstanding place of learning," attended by numerous future leaders of Montgomery and south Alabama.

Education was central in the lives of the Beck children. "A permanent aim of my parents," my father recalled in his family history, "was for their children to have every educational or cultural advantage they could afford. There were books, religious and classical, for us to read. . . . After my parents realized I liked to read, they would bring me a book when they made a trip to Montgomery."

My father respected his father, but his great love—so I always heard—was for his mother. I never knew my grandmother on the Beck side, Miss Lessie as she was known; she died when I was a baby, but my father wrote admiringly of her in our history as a woman of multiple talents, whether she was butchering a freshly killed hog or making clothes for her five children. She was also "an excellent doctor in her own right, which was not unusual because her father and brother were both country doctors." She was the principal disciplinarian, but if the children "could convince her [that we really needed something], be it a piece of clothing, a trip, the use of a car or whatever, she devoted all of her efforts to seeing it was done. She was our champion and Daddy's opposition eventually crumbled."

One side of my grandmother that I would not have known without my father's handwritten family history was her closeness with money—perhaps a reaction to the self-indulgence of her husband, Mr. M. L. Recalling that on the family's semi-annual shopping trips to Troy, a child under twelve could ride the train for half fare, my father wrote, "My mother was one of the most honest persons I ever knew, and yet it was a constant source of wonder how long I was able to ride for half fare. If the conductor was acquainted with Mama he did not make an issue of my age, but occasionally a strange conductor would tangle with my mother and eventually force her to pay up for me. Forevermore that conductor was a scoundrel to her." On arriving in Troy, the children would try on shoes and clothes at one of the town's leading merchants, "but Mama would pretend the price was too high." The family would then troop up to a rival merchant's store and go through the same procedure. She "knew the clerks and they knew her," and she "played off one against the other. They would bargain and haggle over the price and eventually we [would] go home with new clothes." My father's own legendary closeness with money was perhaps partly inspired by memories of those childhood shopping trips.

The years after World War I were good ones for the Becks of Glenwood. "Money was easier," my father wrote, and automobiles were becoming common. "Even [Henry] Ford put a self-starter on his car." I believe that, like many a young man, my father first became skeptical of some of the strictures of religion during his college years, in the mid- to late 1920s, rejoicing in trivial violations of religious dogma while at the same time wanting to set himself apart from his rural roots. Women, he wrote approvingly, "bobbed their hair, in spite of the preachers," and drinking bootlegged liquor was common in cities, although "the small town bumpkins were still restrained by the strict teaching in the churches as well as their lack of sophistication."

I smile every time I read his somewhat snooty reference to small-town bumpkins who lacked sophistication; after all, he was himself a college student not long out of small town Glenwood when he formed those worldly impressions!

"Everything was rolling along merrily," he wrote, "and then all of a sudden, the Depression."

I heard about the Depression on many, many occasions—whether as a somber reminiscence or as a reminder to put aside something for the inevitable rainy day. It clearly was a life-changing event for my father. "No one who did not experience the Great Depression can ever realize the traumatic experiences its victims went through," he wrote. "It was insidious in its early development. Rural merchants and farmers began to feel its effect as early as the middle of the late 1920s. . . . Then came the great stock Market Crash. Our communities had no stock market losses and we made jokes about people jumping out of windows on Wall Street. Then we realized that cotton was six cents a pound, corn fifty cents a bushel, timber four dollars a thousand. Credit, non-existent."

Some of the earliest stories I heard about my father's law practice in those Depression years concerned his battles with the banks. Their determination to foreclose on homes and farms in Crenshaw and Coffee counties was "the most frightening thing happening . . . The man of the house was humiliated. Young people were fearful they would never be able to get a job. The government . . . advocated loans to big corporations and railroads with the idea that it would trickle down to the masses, but these companies used the money to help their desperate financial affairs and unemployment grew, breadlines grew longer and gloom settled over the land. Then Roosevelt was elected and there was the New Deal."

Foster Beck was a lifelong Democrat. He was also a racial progressive, at least by the standards of the times. I distinctly remember him taking me aside when he got home from work—by then we lived in Montgomery—on the day in 1954 that the U.S. Supreme Court decided the school desegregation case. "Son," he said, "The court was right to decide it this way. There will be some high talk, but you are not to engage in it."

He was right about the high talk. It was after that Supreme Court decision that the worst white Alabamians began openly speaking of their hatred for "niggers," and even some white moderates flew Confederate battle flags and demanded the impeachment of Chief Justice Earl Warren. Many Americans remember what followed: the bombing of Martin Luther King, Jr.'s Montgomery home, the savage beatings of the Freedom Riders at the bus station in Montgomery, the rise of George Wallace. In view of the climate of fear in those days, it is perhaps understandable that my father, to my knowledge, did not often talk publicly about his controversial defense of a black-on-white rape case fifteen years earlier in a small town eighty-five miles southeast of Montgomery.

Nevertheless, he took stances involving race that made an

impression on me. For example, I remember, as a twelve-year-old boy, sitting where I had been told to sit, on a flour bin in the kitchen behind a closed swing door, and overhearing him angrily reprimand a newspaper reporter in the next room for his ugly remark about the "all-nigger choir" that had been asked to sing at Mr. M. L.'s funeral in Glenwood. Another time, when I was eleven, he took me to a Montgomery Rebels baseball game in which the first black players in our league would be playing for the visiting Jacksonville Braves. There were predictions of violence at the baseball field and some nasty shouts—I could hear them easily because we sat on the third base side, right behind the Jacksonville dugout, to show our support for the black players—and the taunts grew louder when a black player came out of the dugout and stood in the on-deck circle, then moved to the plate. The home crowd eventually fell silent after one of the black men got two hits, one a double that rattled the scoreboard. I remember my father saying, after the game, "Son, I don't think we will get to see him next year in Montgomery," and sure enough, Hank Aaron was called up to the Milwaukee Braves for the next season.

The racial tension at the ball field that day in Montgomery would not have been new to my father, and I wonder if it took him back to his first meeting with Charles White, Alias, in Kilby prison, where he was being held, pending trial, for his safety. Unlike when Mr. White testified in court, no stenographer was present to record their words at Kilby prison, so I have to surmise what was said from what eventually transpired and from what I remember my father telling me about that meeting. Suffice it to say, the demanding man defended by my father was not at all like the deferential Tom Robinson represented by Atticus Finch in *To Kill a Mockingbird*.

Chapter 5

THE AIR in the Negro ward at Kilby was damp from years of plumbing leaks, backed-up sewage, and the sweat and breathing of its crowded captives. Foster gagged on the stink of urine, excrement, rotted food, and unwashed bodies.

"You gotta bail me outta here, lawyer," Charles White demanded right off the bat, in a rude tone Foster had never heard used by a colored man addressing a white. Charles White was from Detroit and Chicago, not from the South, and his attitude showed it.

"Bail's already been denied, Charles. Sentencing's in three weeks, but I hope to have it all worked out before that."

Charles White glared at him. Foster guessed that Charles must have weighed upward of 275 pounds, close to twice his own weight. Maybe five inches taller. Late forties to mid-fifties. A burly, dark black Negro. Scowling and stinking. "It didn't happen the way she said."

"I can argue all that when we ask for a lighter sentence, Charles—"

"*Shee-uh,*" Charles White interrupted. There were no chairs for the Negro prisoners who had lined up to see their families behind the mesh screen of heavy steel. Charles had to squat to make eye contact with his appointed lawyer, who had been given a low stool on the visitors' side of the screen. The only other white person in the holding pen was a guard armed with a double-barreled shotgun, a measure that struck Foster as ridiculous. He was more afraid of the guard accidentally discharging his shotgun than of the manacled colored men squatting behind the thick steel mesh. And he certainly was not afraid of the Negro women and children on his side of the screen, wailing and moaning for the fifteen minutes they were allowed to visit.

Having expressed his contempt for his lawyer, Charles White leaned his head back and stared at the prison ceiling stained in shades of brown, yellow, and olive, the residue from years of mildew, leaks, and worse.

"You want to tell me what did happen?" As soon as the words came out of his mouth, Foster almost wished he could retract them. Why go into whatever happened? There was not going to be a trial on guilt. Charles already had confessed.

For a flickering moment, Charles White looked at him as if he were looking at another human being; however, he did not reply.

"Charles, you say it didn't happen the way she says. But then why'd you sign that confession?"

"You don't know? They say I don't sign, they turn around and take me straight back to Troy that night. They say I'm dyin' on a rope that night. If I sign, they promise I can stay here in this place till the trial, then I can come back here to serve out my sentence."

"Who promised?"

"Five white men. Sheriff, deputy, three others."

"Maybe we can suppress the confession on the ground it was coerced. But if we succeed, the state may try to seek the death penalty. Are you all right with a life sentence?"

"I don't want to go to jail for life for something I didn't do."

"If you plead in exchange for a promise of life, not the chair, at least you will be alive—"

"Not how I want to live," Charles White said, bouncing on the balls of his feet. Foster guessed Charles was getting tired of squatting in order to look him in the eye, and he thought about standing up, but he didn't.

"Charles, I may be able to bargain for less time than life. And make you eligible for parole." Again, Foster almost wished he could retract. He had never tried to bargain for less than life with eligibility for parole in a capital case. He would have to research it.

"I'm not entering a plea of guilty. I want that confession suppressed," Charles White said, staring at his seated lawyer. Foster was surprised Charles even knew what a plea was, much less a motion to suppress.

"Well, I think that'll be up to the judge whether to suppress but—"

"Do something for me, lawyer," Charles White interrupted, no longer squatting, towering over his seated lawyer like a dark storm.

Foster pushed back on his stool and found his feet. He was still almost half a foot shorter than his client, but it was Charles's mental toughness, not his physique, that left him intimidated and uncertain. This man—if he was going to represent him—was not a grateful, churchgoing colored client from Enterprise who needed his help fighting a foreclosure by the bank, but a strapping, sassy Northern black who had already confessed to raping a white girl and was now demanding a trial, even if it meant the state could ask for the death penalty. Though he was also a man, according to the United States Constitution, entitled to a lawyer. He did not like Charles White, but that was not the point. The point was to give the man good representation, convince him to enter a plea, get him as short a sentence as he could, a chance someday for parole. That could be worked out privately, in chambers, without Judge Parks or a jury ever having to look at, much less listen to, Charles White.

Chapter 6

AS WAS TYPICAL of Southerners in the 1940s and 1950s, I grew up hearing a lot of history about my family, and not only the Beck side. My mother—at the time of the trial, one of several ladies my father was seeing—was from Rayfield and Stewart stock. The Alabama Rayfields fought for the Confederacy, I was told, but the Alabama Stewarts had refused, and so of course I heard stories about that.

One favorite was that because my maternal great-grandfather Rayfield lost a leg during the Civil War, he couldn't plow or hunt, and was of no use, just another mouth to feed. The children were too little to reach the plow handles, so great-grandmother Rayfield plowed the spring corn.

Cora Rayfield, the seventh of eight Rayfield children, eventually caught the eye of Oscar Stewart, a bookish, scientifically inclined young man from nearby Weogufka, Alabama. Because Oscar Stewart's father had refused to serve in the Confederate Army—seeing no point in fighting to own slaves he did not own—the Stewart family was spared the worst of Reconstruction and prospered relative to most.

That made all the Stewarts damn Scalawags and Republicans, in the opinion of some of the Rayfields; but, aware of all the land the Yankees had let the Stewart family keep in and around Weogufka, they consented to the marriage. In the fullness of time, Cora and Oscar Stewart produced seven children, five of whom—Bertha Mae, Abraham Lincoln, William Seward, John Oscar, and Mary—survived. The closest real town (for there was not much to Weogufka) was a day's trip there and back, but the Stewart family rarely needed store-bought goods, with more than two hundred rocky acres of corn, apple and pear orchards, a large, bountiful garden filled with peas, okra, beans, and tomatoes, two fishponds, and sixty acres reserved as pasture for their several dozen cows, sheep, goats, and two mules. There was also a very talented horse that pulled Oscar Stewart's buggy by memory around his rural mail route each morning while Oscar read the *Atlanta Constitution* and studied the Bible.

Oscar carried the mail because it paid a regular government check and didn't take even half a day, but his first love was animal husbandry, especially the latest genetics of chicken breeding, and as soon as he finished the mail route, he turned to his scientific books, manuals, and paraphernalia. Bertha, his oldest, did not regard her father as a warm, loving man, but, like her mother, she was in awe of his intelligence. Oscar returned the admiration, seeing in Bertha someone much like him—curious, bookish—and so he insisted she go to the University of Alabama. Bertha's fondest memory of Papa was over the Christmas holidays of her junior year, the sheer delight that came into his eyes as he hungrily paged through her biology textbook. On returning to Tuscaloosa, she was not surprised to discover that Papa had used his straight razor to remove a page of the book depicting a nude man.

Bertha Stewart had come to the university as the valedictorian of Weogufka High School, but she was far behind the freshmen from the big-city schools of Mobile, Montgomery, and Birmingham, and could only muster C's and an occasional B her first year. Through hard study, sheer grit, and no social life, she caught up and was a straight-A student her final two years, grades that earned her a job as the high school English teacher in Eclectic, Alabama, not far from Weogufka. It was in Eclectic that Bertha met Frances Beck, the two of them sharing a bedroom at a farmhouse on the edge of town. Room and board plus ninety dollars a month was all the compensation the county school board could afford in 1936.

Frances Beck had majored in chemistry and biology at the Woman's College of Alabama in Montgomery (today's Huntingdon College), but the Eclectic school board felt the sciences should be taught by a man, so Frances—a skilled athlete who could throw a football or a baseball like a man—was assigned to teach home economics and physical education to the girls at the high school.

One afternoon, as the two of them walked from school back to the farmhouse, Frances told Bertha about a letter she had received from her brother. Foster wrote that they were looking for teachers in Enterprise, Frances said. She had been feeding Bertha tidbits of information about Foster for months, seeing in her well-read housemate a good match for her similarly bookish brother. On the other hand, the two were different in ways Frances thought might appeal to Foster. If he tended to brood and worry, Bertha was an optimist by nature. He loved history, she loved poetry. While Foster was cautious with money—understandable in view of their father, Mr. M. L., who was not—Bertha didn't hesitate to spend what little she had, though only, she insisted, on "the finer things." Foster was always weighing the ethical answers to this and that, even though he didn't darken the door of a church very often, while Bertha went to church regularly but had a wild side, having once danced the Charleston on a table at a party in Montgomery. Bertha would be a tonic for Foster, who, Frances suspected, had inherited a touch of their daddy's melancholia, but who, unlike Mr. M. L, would not medicate with alcohol or cocaine. The need for teachers in Enterprise spurred Frances to propose that they apply and move there if offered jobs.

Chapter 7

"WHERE *IS* ENTERPRISE," Bertha wanted to know.

Frances was happy to explain: in Coffee County, one county over from Crenshaw, where she and Foster grew up. In *south* Alabama, Frances said proudly. Bertha would love it down there.

It did not take Bertha long after moving to Enterprise to recognize how much she and Foster had in common. "Maybe too much," she told Frances. "We're both awkward socially."

Frances protested.

"And we both read too many books to suit most folks."

Frances thought Bertha had a point there. Those two needed to go to Choctawhatchee Bay for a weekend with fishing poles and no books, Frances told Bertha, but she knew it wouldn't happen, and not just because it wouldn't look right, an unmarried couple. Bertha had tried fishing with Foster on the Conecuh River and hated it.

"We even have similar fathers," Bertha said. "I love Mr. M. L.," she quickly added.

Frances dearly loved her father: for rising above the ordinary men of Crenshaw County; for seeing enough promise in her to send her to college. His bouts of depression and alcoholism, his occasional resort to cocaine, were to Frances only romantic proof of his adventuresome nature. She would concede, however, that some thought him crazy.

"Papa's even crazier," Bertha said. "Naming his first-born son Abraham Lincoln Stewart. Sending a pillow to that Eugene Debs in the Atlanta penitentiary."

Frances did not think much of Bertha's father sending a pillow to the Socialist Party leader Debs, but she could not help being amused by his naming his Alabama son Abraham Lincoln. It was no wonder Bertha's brother had moved to Fitzgerald, Georgia (founded by Union and Confederate veterans), after vet school—where he simply went by "Doc Stewart." Frances had never met Bertha's father, but from what she heard, he was not at all like her own father. Mr. Stewart did not drink or use drugs, did not swear, and he read the Bible every day on his mail route. Bertha's story about her father razor-blading the naked man's picture out of her biology book fit Frances's image of Mr. Stewart. Just the opposite of Mr. M. L.

I HEARD MY MOTHER say more than once that "Foster saw prettier girls"—that as a single, up-and-coming lawyer, "there were opportunities," and not only in Enterprise but in Dothan, Eufaula, Mobile. Maybe so, but she must have grown on him. He often said when I was a teenager that she embodied the word "quality"; she appealed to his serious nature. She was almost regal, with her erect bearing, graceful neck, long straight black hair, and calm blue eyes that widened and sparkled when she became excited. And when she spoke he actually found himself listening, unlike his experience with other girls.

She was Alabama born and raised but not ensnared by and mired in Alabama. She dreamed of travel to New York, even Europe. When she talked with fervor about the poetry of Emily Dickinson or proudly showed him her daintily inscribed college notes on *King Lear*, he had to smile at her genuine emotion. And for all of her schoolteacherish ways, she had once fired a shotgun off the back porch into the pitch-black woods behind her rural Weogufka home to scare a screech owl that was keeping her mama, Miss Cora, awake. To the amusement of her brothers, the unlucky owl was found lying dead on the ground the next morning. All the same, my father did not bring up marriage in 1938, let alone propose. "He was not ready," Mother said, when I asked why they had dated so long before getting married.

My mother was the only woman my father talked to about the Charles White case: about what he was going to do.

THE FIRST TIME they talked about it, they were sitting together on the front porch of the boardinghouse in Enterprise where my mother stayed, a white-painted, wide-planked two-story Victorian bordered by blooming gardenias and surrounded by pecan trees and crepe myrtle. She was sitting on the porch swing and he was sitting next to her in a straw-bottomed chair. He had just begun to tell her about Charles White when he was interrupted. Miss Pauline— Mother's landlady, as I recall her name—was offering iced tea from behind the front screen door. Miss Pauline did not like to open the screen because it let in flies.

"No, thank you, Miss Pauline," Foster said, feeling the statement was really addressed to him. Bertha could open the screen door and go to the icebox for tea anytime she wanted. He had never seen the icebox, never even been inside the house. He didn't want to look at Miss Pauline and start a conversation, but he was afraid she would keep on standing at the screen trying to listen. He decided to lower his voice with Bertha. It was best that Miss Pauline, one of Enterprise's biggest gossips, not hear about Charles White.

"He's signed a full confession in exchange for a promise of a life sentence," he whispered. "All I'll be doing is trying to get him twenty years and a chance for parole, instead of life imprisonment." He did not tell her that Charles wanted the confession suppressed and a trial on guilt or innocence. He still believed he could convince Charles to enter the guilty plea for a reduced sentence and a chance of parole. No need to worry Bertha over a trial, something that was unlikely to come about.

"What's he like?"

"Demanding. I don't like him one bit."

"I suppose the next thing you'll say is it's not relevant whether you like him?"

"It's not relevant to my duty as a lawyer to represent him. But realistically, there's no question his attitude could affect the sentence he gets, that's human nature, especially with a Negro defendant. I will try to work out something in advance, before Charles and the judge meet each other."

"Can you coach him to be obsequious?"

"I'm not sure. He's from up North. Course I've only met him once . . ." His already lowered voice trailed off as he heard the slap of the screen door behind him.

Miss Pauline was holding a tin serving tray, decorated with painted white magnolia blossoms.

"Thank you, ma'am!" Bertha beamed, taking a tall glass, shining golden brown in the afternoon sun. "Ummm! This hits the spot!"

"Thank you, ma'am," Foster mumbled, rising halfway from his chair. A chunk of ice, broken off the block by Miss Pauline with an ice pick, floated to the inside edge of his glass, making it hard for him to sip without spilling. The glass sweated condensation in the heat, making it slippery.

To fill the silence, Miss Pauline wondered how Enterprise would get through the summer with it already this hot in June.

Foster said nothing, so Bertha said, "Well, we'll just have to drink lots of your fine sweet tea, Miss Pauline!" She shot Foster a look that said, I have to get along with my landlady. She was glad that Foster was a serious man who spoke grammatically and made good use of his verbs and adverbs, but she thought he sometimes seemed a little aloof.

"I was just leaving," Foster said, placing his glass of tea on a white wicker side table. "But thank you again, Miss Pauline," he added unconvincingly. "Bertha, can we talk just a minute out front?"

Miss Pauline had been pining to learn what the two were whispering about. She had already tried to eavesdrop from inside before lighting on the strategy of serving the tea. Now she regretted using up two chunks from the ice block for no return. She thought Foster was cold and ill-mannered and wished Bertha had another suitor. She retreated behind the closed screen door. Was Bertha coming in now? Miss Pauline did not want to hold the door open long and let in the flies.

"Just shortly, ma'am," Bertha said.

"I wanted to say something else," Foster said when Miss Pauline had disappeared behind the screen.

"I know."

"The thing is, he ought not to have to be obsequious. The time he spends in prison shouldn't be based on attitudes about race."

"Wouldn't a white defendant need to be polite and humble too?"

"Yes, but it's different. You know how it is."

Of course she knew, though not as well as he did. There were no Negroes in Weogufka—none she knew of in all of Coosa County. The hilly, rocky land that far north in Alabama was not suited for cotton. "I'm beginning to dislike Charles White myself," she said.

Foster shook his head in disapproval.

"You said *you* didn't like him one bit."

"But I said it—" He paused as they both nodded a greeting to an older white man, a neighbor of Miss Pauline's. The man nodded in return to Foster and tipped his hat to Bertha before continuing on his business. "I said it because of his attitude. I wanted him to be grateful. Now I'm the one who wants *his* respect."

"Is that why you're doing it?"

Foster put off a direct answer. The fact was, he was doing it because he could not refuse to represent Charles White and still believe what he claimed to believe and wanted to believe about law and the Constitution. But instead of all that, which he worried would sound pious and self-centered, he said, "I was asked because all the Troy lawyers came up with excuses. Everybody knows that. So in a way, no one can hold it against me."

"And the judge asked you, of all the other lawyers in south Alabama, because you are Mr. M. L.'s son."

He resisted the thought. "And not because I'm a great trial lawyer?"

Both of them laughed and Bertha squeezed his hand. People

said Foster had no sense of humor, but she said that was unfair: he laughed at human folly; he teased her in ways she usually found affectionate; most of all, he laughed at himself. But he refused to laugh at some of the jokes he was supposed to go along with—vulgar jokes, cruel ones—and that refusal got him into trouble with the men who told those jokes.

Chapter 8

MY MOTHER WORRIED about the effect on my father's modest law practice if word got around about the Charles White case. If he insisted on seeking a short sentence and parole for an admitted Negro rapist, it should be for his own independent reasons, not because of his daddy. But she would have to be careful raising the question so as not to give offense to the great man in the eyes of his son.

My father's relationship with his father was complex. The monthly round trips from Montgomery to Glenwood that my father dutifully insisted on making when I was a child speak louder than words of his devotion. Two of the letters he wrote his father on his birthday provide some additional insight into that relationship.

His first letter, postmarked June 1936, and written on his law firm stationery, begins by recalling the good times and lessons learned on their camping and fishing trips, reminiscences that, while sincere, were likely intended to bring some cheer to his moody, often depressed father. But he must have known that resorting to senti- mentality would not be sufficient to that task, for his letter shifts in tone—to the kind of subtle flattery that might have appealed to Mr. M. L. Unless "the elders," my father wrote, "transmitted their experiences to succeeding generations, mistakes that could have been avoided would be repeated time after time. [The Creek Indian Nation] had their elder council to expound their philosophies and to counsel and advise the impetuous and active younger warriors. Voltaire drew students and rulers alike to seek knowledge at his feet. Jefferson directly influenced the nation long after he actively retired. But things like that seem to be the exception now."

These thoughts were repeated nine years later in another birthday letter, this one dated June 1945, written from Fort McPherson in Atlanta not long before my father was discharged from the army. "In the old days before books and printing, the elders were looked to for a philosophy of life. Their words, based on their experiences, were valued because from them their children learned how to cope with life. . . . It seems now we don't have time for such. Books have taught us much of the mechanics of living, but we seem to lack a satisfactory philosophy of life. As a result younger generations will have to make the same mistakes over and over. Maybe that is the implacable law of life," my father pessimistically wrote, before concluding, on a lighter note, that having looked "all over Atlanta for a shirt large enough," he would be sending his father only some socks as a birthday present.

I don't think it is reading too much between the lines to suggest, from those letters, that my father not only respected his father but also wanted to please him—and perhaps impress him. If that is so, it is no wonder that my mother worried that my father was taking on the Charles White case because of his daddy.

———

"ALL THE SAME, I hope you aren't taking this Charles White case because of Mr. M. L.," Bertha cautioned as they continued their stroll from Miss Pauline's.

"Daddy's got nothing to do with what I'm doing or not doing about Charles White," Foster said. He knew that was a bit of a lie. He could not escape who he was and how he was raised. Born legally blind in one eye and weakened by diphtheria as a baby, the smallest of the five children to survive and a favorite of his mother simply *because* he survived, he had been a shy, serious child, in awe of the tall, strapping, garrulous man that townspeople and visitors alike called Mr. M. L. As an adult, Foster had come to be proud of his father's intellect and open-mindedness, while deploring his abuse of alcohol, so much so that he barely touched liquor himself.

"Besides, Bertha, you've got enough to worry about with your own job. Did you ever talk to the superintendent, find out what he wants?" The superintendent, a powerful man in Enterprise, where Bertha was the high school English teacher, had presided over Coffee County's schools, white and colored, for more than thirty years. Foster had heard from Frances that Bertha was under pressure from the superintendent about something, and he was trying to change the subject.

"He wants a better grade for his grandson. I can't let him make me, but I have to keep my job."

Foster knew she had to, and not just for the small salary. Bertha had to keep her job as a teacher. Teaching was what got her wrought up; Bertha believed in teaching Coffee County high school boys and girls *King Lear* and *Great Expectations* and Byron, Shelley, and Keats the way he believed in defending their parents against the banks. Foster suspected that not even a proposal of marriage would keep Bertha in Enterprise unless she could teach.

They had walked three blocks from Miss Pauline's and into the colored section of Enterprise. Foster smiled and nodded hello to an older Negro man, who tipped his hat to Bertha and stepped aside to make room for the white couple to pass. The man was one of a small number of Coffee County Negroes who actually owned the land he farmed, one of an even smaller number of Foster's clients, white or colored, who paid him in cash for his legal work. Foster had taken great pleasure the previous year in turning away the bank's effort to foreclose on the man's farm.

Foster's thoughts returned to Bertha. If she didn't give the superintendent what he wanted for his grandson, she might get fired and would quickly run out of money. He knew she saved little from her teacher's salary, half of which she was already sending to her mother in Weogufka, and that she was spending too much of what was left on the Book-of-the-Month Club, explaining, when he asked how she could afford so many of the Club's selections, that she wanted to "learn what to read from the smart people in New York." The exception was poetry, about which she felt confident enough to buy on her own.

"You know, the superintendent's been in the education field quite some time," Foster said. "Surely he knows a thing or two about grading an English paper."

Bertha did not reply.

"Well, then, if you won't budge, I guess we'll both wind up in the poorhouse," he said, impulsively taking her hand, still hoping to persuade her to give the boy a satisfactory grade.

"Well then yourself, Foster Beck," Bertha said, freeing her hand. He had no business hint-hinting what to do about her boss, and he knew it. And it was unfair for him to tell her what to do to keep her job while at the same time risking his own career over the Charles White case.

"Foster. Your family's already done more than anyone in south Alabama for the colored." She wanted to end the talk of the superintendent and return to the perils of representing an admitted Negro rapist.

Foster wasn't sure if it was true that his family had done all that much for the colored, but he knew what she really meant and why she said it. He paused, watching three young boys—two white, one black—playing football. Then he said, "Bertha, I'm going to take it on. It's about what the law requires of a lawyer, not about Daddy. For all I know, Daddy might not even want me to take it."

"You'll be very unpopular taking this case."

Foster almost said what he thought: a lawyer who had any self-respect would put popularity aside. But he suppressed that thought, convinced it would come out sounding pompous and self–righteous. Instead he said, "Maybe I'll be unpopular, but there's not much risk of that. Charles White signed a full confession, so there's no need to have a public trial over whether he did it. But the state can't use the confession and still ask for the electric chair, so the only question is whether he's sentenced to life imprisonment or whether I can get him less time and a chance for parole. I'll negotiate for that in private, in Judge Parks's chambers. There won't be any need for a public trial."

The boy playing quarterback overthrew his receiver, the ball bouncing into the dirt road. Foster picked up the ball and, as his sister Frances had taught him, threw a perfect spiral. The three boys, obviously surprised that the slight, bespectacled man could throw a spiral at all, much less accurately, acknowledged the feat with respectful "awwhh"s before resuming their game.

"So he really *is* guilty?" Bertha said. "He signed a confession."

Foster thought about how to reply to that. Charles White was a big man, but he had been arrested in a small Southern town, then rushed in a car full of white lawmen with guns to Montgomery before he could be lynched. Charles hadn't admitted to being scared, but even with all his arrogance and size and being from the North, he had to have been one scared Negro when they offered to keep him safe in Kilby prison instead of taking him back to Troy that night and a likely lynching, then proposed giving him a life sentence instead of the electric chair. But only if he confessed—meaning the confession might be false, or partly false? When he'd asked Charles what had actually happened, all he'd said was, "It wasn't like she said"—not exactly a denial. Maybe he took some kind of advantage of her and now was trying to blame her? It was not, after all, unusual for a criminal to recant, or at least try to mitigate, a confession.

"Like most of the rest of us, my clients usually aren't purely innocent or purely guilty, Bertha. Something improper may have gone on between them. I don't know exactly what. The fact is, even if it wasn't rape, it's not something a Negro needs to be talking about to a white jury. And he won't have to. It won't be tried. I'll negotiate the best plea deal I can for him and be done with it."

But for the first time, he was beginning to have some doubts. Charles White had sounded pretty strong when he told him there could be no plea deal; he wanted to go to trial. Foster was thinking that maybe Charles really was innocent, and had been forced by the threat of the lynch rope that night to admit to a crime he did not commit.

Chapter 9

SOUTHERNERS were like an ethnic group back when I was growing up, with our own version of history, our particular grievances, our preferred preparations of foods, our unique accents. Like other American ethnic groups, we had our rituals, especially in small towns and rural areas. At least as late as the late 1940s and early 1950s, there was, in parts of the South, an annual rite called Confederate Grave Decoration Day.

I recall hearing that my father received a surprise visit from a Pike County court official on a Confederate Grave Decoration Day event held in Crenshaw County. If that event was held on the first Sunday in July—the preferred date for some Protestant denominations—then, based on the 1938 calendar, the visit from the Pike County court official would have occurred on the afternoon of July 3.

There would be a few firecrackers on Monday, July 4, but Independence Day was not as festive an occasion in south Alabama as up North. For many in south Alabama, the Fourth was a Yankee holiday, celebrating a successful rebellion. By comparison, Confederate Grave Decoration Day commemorated what was, for many Southern whites, a failed rebellion, a noble but misunderstood lost cause.

Initially, the day was observed in places such as Glenwood as a way of honoring the fallen and upholding some shred of pride. After a few years of just decorating graves, however, Glenwood's Confederate widows reasoned that as long as they were all going to be together, they might as well share food and recipes and bring along their children to romp and play. Since Confederate Grave Decoration Day was held on a Sunday afternoon in a church cemetery, it was only natural that afternoon preaching and singing were soon included.

The Becks were members of the Methodist church; Mr. M. L. had donated the lumber for the new church building. But for events such as the first Sunday in July, he favored the Glenwood Hard Shell Baptist Church.

The Hard Shell Baptist Church and adjoining cemetery, located on a forlorn dirt road outside Glenwood, a quarter mile from the Conecuh River, were surrounded by cypress trees, volunteer oaks, and other hardwoods, and also by scattered young, second-growth pines that would not be ready to cut for another twenty years, assuming they thrived in the swampy terrain. The church building was an unadorned, whitewashed wooden structure that rested on stacks of river rocks, high enough off the ground to remain dry each spring when the Conecuh overflowed its banks, and to allow small children, dogs, and rattlesnakes to crawl around underneath. Inside, there were several dozen carved hardwood pews, a simple altar, and a wooden podium. A choir of twenty women ranging in age from young teens to grandmothers, along with a few balding men, sat behind the podium, beneath an unpainted wooden cross that had split in a couple of places as the pine wood dried out over the years. There were always more people than seats on the first Sunday in July, but no one had to remain standing for long because worshipers, having made their appearance, were only too happy to relinquish their places on the hard pews and join the others standing around eating and talking under the magnolias and water oaks in the yard outside.

The service was led by Brother Ed, a hard-fat, bald man in his fifties who preached against liquor, the Pope, card playing, dancing, and painted faces, and who exuded fiery passion more than love. From time to time, younger men, some of them itinerant preachers, some just laymen, would relieve Brother Ed during the all-day service. In these intervals, Brother Ed was hard to find.

My father knew that his father preferred the Hard Shell Baptists on the first Sunday to what he called "those blue-nosed Methodists," and he knew why: Mr. M. L. had developed a special friendship over the years with Brother Ed. As a teenager, my father would observe Brother Ed coming to the house in the late afternoons. He and Mr. M. L. would retire to the study, close the sliding pocket door, and after a while come out in a jolly mood to sit on the porch and smoke Virginia cheroots. My father wrote in our family history that he would slip into the study before the maid came and smell the empty glasses with a few grains of sugar left in the bottom and understand what they had been up to. In those days, my father explained, Alabama was a dry state, but Florida was wet until national Prohibition. An Alabama law called the Two Quarts Law said an Alabama man could order two quarts of whiskey a month from Florida for his needs. Mr. M. L.'s needs were not met by two quarts, and as a boy, my father would find whiskey cartons addressed to Brother Ed and other supposed teetotalers.

Not seeing his father or Brother Ed—who had been temporarily relieved from his preaching duties—Foster assumed the two of them had slipped out into the woods for a slug of Four Roses. He turned his attention to Bertha.

The line for food—having paused to allow an enfeebled veteran of the War Between the States to cut in and fill his plate—was beginning to move again. Foster took Bertha's elbow and carefully guided her around the smoking fire pits, where thick, juicy sides of beef and sugar-cured pork had been slow-cooking over hickory since before midnight, and handed her a thick, cream-colored platter from a stack at the head of the line. The tables placed end to end, a good seventy-five feet in their combined length, swayed under the cast-iron pots and kettles heaped with sweet corn, string beans, little white Glenwood peas, and fried okra, all harvested the previous fall and put up in mason jars. There were also early tomatoes and fresh okra, large bowls of stuffed eggs, camp stew, rice dishes, fruit salads, casseroles, turnip greens, fried chickens, sliced breads, and all manner of fresh-baked pies, cakes, and cookies, the competing fragrances of smoked meat and fresh pastry creating a sensory delirium. To drink, there were big zinc tubs of lemonade for the children and sweet tea for the grownups, both beverages cooled by chunks from the two-hundred-pound block of ice fetched that morning from the icehouse in Luverne. Thirty or more round-top trunks used by the ladies to bring the food they had cooked were set in a neat row off to the sides, their lids closed to keep out the flies. Each trunk was marked by a special colored ribbon so its owner could find hers quickly whenever one of her platters or pots on the tables began to run low, but the identifying ribbons were hardly necessary as the ladies mostly stood like sentinels right behind their respective trunks, nodding and smiling encouragement to the men as they appraised each dish. The ladies pretended to inquire this or that of one another, but they never really took their eyes off the tables.

"We left off Confederate and called it just Grave Decoration

Day, but we did this at our Presbyterian cemetery in Weogufka, same sort of thing," Bertha said. She always stood up for her hometown, defensive of it because Foster acted like Weogufka was in north Alabama and hillbilly, even though all you had to do was look at a map to see that Weogufka was smack in the center of the state. "'Cept we did it first Sunday in May, not July. You see, Foster," she said, smiling and softening her tone, "it's not really about the War. It's a competition among the ladies to see who goes home with the least leftovers."

Bertha tried her best, but she was not much of a cook and was cheerfully unapologetic about her failing. Having a sweet tooth, she had made and brought a peach cobbler, which, as the contribution of a newcomer to Enterprise, was relegated to the far end of the row of tables. Foster was the first one to take a slice, having loyally saved room on his plate.

"Where's Mr. M. L.?" Bertha asked Frances, as she and Foster strolled up to a tall magnolia. The lower limbs had been cut off years ago, leaving room to sit under the tree in the shade. The Becks had reserved a family space by laying out flowered quilts on the bare, swept ground. Frances was seated beside Delmas, her serious beau, who had come all the way from Meridian, Mississippi. As always, Frances was in high spirits.

Frances giggled and winked at her blushing brother. She said she expected Mr. M. L. and Brother Ed were praying over something out in the woods.

Frances did not tease her brother in Bertha's presence out of meanness; she loved him, and wanted the best for him. As youngsters growing up in Glenwood, the two had been great friends, secretly picking cotton when they needed money for something forbidden, receiving a dollar per hundred pounds. Frances could outpick Foster, a hundred pounds to seventy, as a six-year-old girl, and outrun and outwrestle him as late as their teens, when their mother put a stop to it. Frances suspected she could still outpick, outrun, and outwrestle her brother. She knew he'd had no dates in high school, and, from all she could learn, few in college. Ever since law school, though, Foster had been viewed as something of a catch, and she suspected he was enjoying playing the field for the first time in his life. Frances had wanted him to have that, but now he was thirty-two, time to settle down, and she had handpicked the lively Bertha.

After embarrassing her brother by telling about their daddy drinking whiskey in the woods beside the church with Brother Ed, Frances decided that Foster and Bertha should have some time to themselves. Taking Delmas by the hand, she walked over to the zinc tub for more sweet iced tea. That was when she noticed for the first time the tall, slender stranger from the court in Pike County, who asked if she was Miss Frances.

Impressed that he had driven on a Sunday to Confederate Grave Decoration Day just to see her brother, Frances proudly escorted the stranger to the place where Foster and—she hoped—her future sister-in-law were still sitting quietly on the flowered quilts under the magnolia. Although Frances wanted them to have some time alone, she now wished they were not sitting by themselves, as she wanted many others to hear of a visitor who came all the way from Troy to see her brother. For what, she had no idea, but surely it was some-thing important.

The man from Troy tipped his hat to Miss Bertha before asking for just a brief word with Mr. Foster.

| Chapter 10

THE VISITOR FROM TROY apparently did not say much on Confederate Grave Decoration Day, just that Judge Parks wanted to see counsel in chambers—as best I can determine, on July 5, the day after the federal holiday. Trying to piece together what occurred before that day, I can only surmise that Charles White steadfastly refused to allow my father to negotiate a plea deal in exchange for a life sentence with the possibility of parole, disavowed his confession, insisted he was innocent, and demanded a trial. I surmise this because the confession was not used (or referred to other than that one time in the *Troy Messenger* article) and because of what later transpired in court.

What became of the confession? I have been unable to locate a motion to suppress, but such a motion almost surely was made. Suppression of the confession was apparently wanted by Charles White, and filing such a motion would not have foreclosed later negotiations for less than a life sentence—although my cautious father would have warned his client of the risk that the state might seek death if the motion were granted.

Assuming a motion to suppress was filed, it is possible that the state would not have opposed it, even assuming there were grounds to do so. A decision by the court to suppress—*not* to allow use of the confession, to try Charles White on guilt, on whether he'd raped the white girl or not—meant that the state could seek the death penalty, something it could not do if it used a confession that it procured with a promise of life imprisonment. Once Solicitor Ewell ("E. C.") Orme knew he was up against a green young attorney who wasn't from Troy, perhaps he welcomed such a motion, figuring he could win a conviction without the confession, convince the jury to recommend death, and send Charles White to the electric chair.

Whatever the reason that the confession was not used, I think the revelation that the state would seek the death penalty came during that meeting in early July in the chambers of Judge Parks, located upstairs in the Pike County courthouse, in an office with four tall windows that looked out over the town. Here's how I believe it must have transpired.

JUDGE PARKS assured Foster the confession was inadmissible and could not be referred to; the law was clear on that. Having disposed of the confession, Judge Parks proceeded to deny Foster's motion to quash the indictment because no Negroes had been on the grand jury. The Scottsboro case didn't require that, only that they be called for *possible* service. Was there anything else before setting the trial date?

"I want to discuss a reduced sentence, an opportunity for eventual parole, that I can take back to my client," Foster said, turning as he spoke to Solicitor Orme.

Solicitor E. C. Orme was an older man who carried himself with authority, proud of his unusual height. Referring to Foster as "son," Solicitor Orme winked at Judge Parks and said that no, son, there would be no plea deal. The state wanted the death penalty.

Foster needed air, but he couldn't just get up and walk outside. He had hoped and believed up until that moment that something short of life imprisonment could be worked out. Instead, a man's life was now in his hands. The confidence he had gained by winning civil cases for the poor against the rapacious banks, by winning the bastardy case against a powerful family, was draining away fast. This was a capital punishment case, and not some petty theft charge against a sharecropper back in Enterprise.

Solicitor Orme grinned at Judge Parks and said that defense counsel looked like he had just seen a ghost. Turning to Foster, he said, son, your client's going to Hell crispy, fresh out of the electric chair.

Judge Parks ignored the bullying of Foster. He said that Foster had entered an appearance for the accused and could not withdraw, but he would grant him time to prepare.

Foster noted the use of "the accused" instead of "the Nigra." Was the judge trying to signal that he would try the case fairly? Foster knew he could find an excuse or some kind of legal grounds to withdraw, despite Judge Parks's warning. But now his blood was up. "I've got no intention of withdrawing, Judge," he answered reflexively. The fact was, he didn't need to think much: he could not see a way to hold his head up if he abandoned Charles White now, especially after all his big talk to Bertha about the law and the Constitution. "But I want time to see my client about this new development. And I want to see Mary Etta Bray."

Judge Parks said that Etta was being held until her trial in the women's prison near Montgomery, in Tutwiler. He didn't want her lynched either.

There would be no call for lynching a rapist who was on his way to the chair, Solicitor Orme assured Judge Parks. As for Etta, she would go up for life as an accomplice to rape, the least she deserved for luring Miss Elizabeth to her house. Turning to Foster, the solicitor winked and asked, are you thinking about defending Etta too, son?

"Name's Foster Campbell Beck, not son. Maybe I will. Or maybe under the ethical rules, she'll need separate counsel."

Solicitor Orme was on his feet, his tone angry, threatening. He didn't need to be told about any ethics by Mr. Foster Campbell Beck.

Judge Parks chuckled, then calmly admonished both counsel from his swivel chair. He was not wearing his black robe, but in his perfectly starched white shirt and blue silk tie snugged up under his collar, he was, as Foster appraised him, in perfect command of his chambers. He would postpone the trial till the fourteenth; they would strike a jury on the thirteenth. That would give Foster time to see his client again, and Etta to boot.

Before dismissing the lawyers, Judge Parks reminded Solicitor Orme about the second Scottsboro case, two years earlier.

Solicitor Orme said of course, he knew about that second Scottsboro case. There would have to be a couple of colored summoned for the panel. But he still had the right to strike peremptorily as well as for cause.

Foster was not really counting on the Supreme Court's ruling that Negroes had to be called for possible jury selection. It had not made any difference in south Alabama. No sooner was voir dire commenced than the prosecutor would exercise his challenges and get rid of the Negroes. Women didn't serve on Alabama juries either, although maybe it was just as well, Foster thought, recalling the coal-black skin and threatening demeanor of his client. He would have to see the warden at Kilby about getting Charles White washed up and shaved and given a haircut before he was sent to Troy to stand trial.

THE ABILITY of a prosecutor in 1938 Alabama to eliminate African Americans from juries by using peremptory strikes—strikes of a prospective juror without stating a reason—probably comes as no surprise to most people. What may shock, however, is the fact that the practice continued for decades after the Charles White case.

The 1875 Civil Rights Act prohibited states from discriminating in selection of jurors, and in *Strauder v. West Virginia*, 100 U.S. 303 (1879), the United States Supreme Court ruled that a state statute limiting jury service to whites violated the equal protection of the laws guaranteed by the Fourteenth Amendment. Despite that promising beginning, however, and notwithstanding the second Scottsboro case (requiring that blacks be called for possible service on grand juries), many district attorneys continued to use peremptory strikes to eliminate any black person from appearing on a petite—a trial jury—especially for a trial of an African American defendant.

In 1965, almost one hundred years after the *Strauder* decision and more than a quarter century after the Charles White trial, the Supreme Court addressed the precise issue, but not in a satisfactory manner. Despite the fact that all six African Americans on the prospective juror panel had been struck by the prosecutor, the court said that, absent proof of intentional discrimination, there was no constitutional violation (*Swain v. Alabama*, 380 U.S. 202, *re-hearing denied*, 381 U.S. 921 [1965]).

After considerable criticism—e.g., "*Swain v. Alabama*: The Use of Peremptory Challenges to Strike Blacks from Juries," 27 *How. L. J.* 1571 (1984)—the Supreme Court revisited the issue in *Batson v. Kentucky*, 476 U.S. 79 (1986), and overruled *Swain* to the extent that it required proof of intentional discrimination. Where prosecutors methodically eliminated all black jurors through the use of peremptory strikes, the court held that an inference of discrimination would arise, requiring prosecutors to give a non-race-based reason for each strike. Otherwise, the struck potential juror would be placed back on the panel.

Despite this reform, the Equal Justice Initiative, a nonprofit organization headquartered in Montgomery, Alabama, found, in a paper entitled "Illegal Racial Discrimination in Jury Selection: A Continuing Legacy," that twenty years after *Batson*, appellate courts in eight Southern states were still being "forced to recognize continuing problems with racially based jury selection." Indeed, as recently as November 2015 the Supreme Court heard oral argument on a challenge to alleged racially motivated uses of peremptory challenges.

And so, of course, no African Americans survived peremptory challenges for the 1938 trial in *State of Alabama v. Charles White, Alias*.

Chapter 11

L AWYERS, whether they handle litigation or transactions, sometimes receive unpleasant news that must be disclosed to the client. For their part, clients sometimes blame the bringer of the bad news. From what my father told me, his next meeting with Charles White in the colored ward at Kilby was initially pretty tense.

"*Shee-uh,*" Charles White said when his lawyer told him the State would seek the death penalty. "You told me they might if I don't leave that confession alone. Now you seem surprised, lawyer Beck." He gave Foster a contemptuous look through the heavy steel mesh screen that separated them, then rolled his eyes to stare at the discolored ceiling.

"Without your confession," Foster said, "they'll have to prove rape beyond a reasonable doubt."

Charles stopped staring at the ceiling and looked at his lawyer. "I told you it didn't happen like she's sayin'. I told you the only reason I signed that piece of paper was they promised me I wouldn't get the rope that night."

"So, you don't want to die?"

As at their first meeting when Foster asked, "What really happened?" the contempt drained from Charles's face. "What you sayin'?"

"I'm saying, if you want to live, you've got to help me help you."

"You believe me?"

Foster had suspected that question was coming and had resolved to answer right back without a pause, but still he hesitated at the weight of the moment. "It doesn't matter what I believe. All that matters is whether they can prove to all twelve of the jury beyond a reasonable doubt that you raped her."

"Twelve white men."

"Well, yes."

"*Shee-uh*," Charles said, this time more in despair than contempt.

"Troy's not as bad as some places. This is Alabama, not Mississippi. I can imagine what you've heard it's like down here, coming from Detroit."

"Twelve white men from *Dee*-troit wouldn't believe a nigger in a case like this," Charles said. "If you'd *been* anywhere you'd know that much." Charles spat in disgust on the filthy floor, and the white prison guard fingered the trigger of his shotgun. "Anyways, now they want to kill me, I'm gonna say my piece, lawyer Beck. I'm tellin' that jury what really happened."

Foster pursed his lips. "I'm not sure I want you taking the stand."

"Why's that?"

Foster closed his eyes and frowned. "The State can find out if you've been in trouble before. They'll use it on cross-examination if you take the stand."

"No trouble before this."

Foster was not convinced. "If they get papers saying you've been convicted somewhere, served time, they'll put that in your face on the stand, and the jury will believe you're a repeat criminal. That will make them more likely to convict you. But the jury won't know about any prior trouble if you don't testify. And you have a constitutional right not to take the stand."

Charles White did not do him the courtesy of a nod, much less another word. He just glared. Foster imagined with a shudder how this kind of defiance would play to the jury. Even what Charles did for a living was suspicious: reading cards and telling fortunes for money.

After another moment, Foster said, "Besides, it won't be necessary for you to take the stand. I've been doing a little asking around. I talked to someone who talked to Dr. Stewart, the examining physician."

"What'd he say?"

"He said that biologically, she's still a virgin."

Chapter 12

I N 1915, the boll weevil—an insect indigenous to Mexico that destroys cotton bolls before they ripen—stormed into south Alabama, having already ravaged Texas, Louisiana, and Mississippi. Within three years, entire cotton fields had been laid waste. Desperate, south Alabama farmers planted peanuts, a crop that proved to be a godsend: the combination of sandy soil, lots of sunshine, and the imperviousness of the peanut plant to the boll weevil brought prosperity to the region, nowhere more than in and around Enterprise.

This history was told and retold throughout my boyhood—after all, I was born in Enterprise, even though I grew up in Montgomery. What I remember best is the way Enterprise memorialized the boll weevil's contribution. It was even reported in my elementary school *Weekly Reader*, the only mention that I recall of anything about Alabama in any *Weekly Reader*: the true story of the creation and dedication of a sculpture of a female nymph holding over her head a pedestal on which was mounted a much larger-than-life replica of a Mexican boll weevil. The inscription read: "In Profound Appreciation of the Boll Weevil and What it has Done as the Herald of

Prosperity, This Monument was Erected by the Citizens of Enterprise, Coffee County, Alabama." Enterprise's humorous veneration of the boll weevil contrasted with the most famous monument in Troy: a statue of John Wilkes Booth. People said the different monuments illustrated that the distance between Troy and Enterprise was greater than thirty-seven miles.

"Troy's like Babylon," Bertha said. She and Foster were standing in line outside the Methodist church in Enterprise, waiting their turn to shake hands with the preacher. Bertha was alluding to the sermon they had just heard, which praised Daniel for gaining permission from his Babylonian captors to forgo the meat and wine apportioned him by King Nebuchadnezzar and take only the food and water consistent with his faith. "Compared to Troy, Enterprise is Jerusalem," Bertha said.

"Bertha, you've never even been to Troy." Foster's tone was impatient. Bertha had made him waste part of his Sunday morning, convincing him to come to church with her by talking up the visiting minister, an Emory theology school graduate. In Foster's opinion, the sermon had not been worth the sacrifice.

"True," Bertha admitted, as they strolled from the Methodist church toward the commercial center of Enterprise. "I haven't been to Troy, but I can contrast it with Enterprise just by their monuments. Enterprise has its boll weevil. Troy has that awful statue of John Wilkes Booth. I don't need to go to Troy to see it. I've read and heard all about it. It's the only one in the nation, North or South, Foster."

"Troy's still not Babylon, and I'm not Daniel," he interrupted, heading off an anticipated analogy to the lion's den and his upcoming defense of Charles White. When Bertha remained silent, he pursued it. "You are uninformed about Troy, Bertha. That monument to John Wilkes Booth was not commissioned by the town and never was installed on public property. I think you missed the point."

"And I think *you* missed the point, Foster." Now it was Bertha who was interrupting. "Daniel, a slave, triumphed over mighty King Nebuchadnezzar. And I thought you would like that, the underdog winning over a king."

Winning over king or a judge, Foster thought—only now, a jury as well. He decided this was as good a time as there was going to be to bring up the dramatic change in the case of *State of Alabama v. Charles White, Alias.* "You remember my telling you about the Troy case, the alleged rape?" He knew she remembered. He knew that was why she brought up Troy being like Babylon; she was still hoping to talk him out of taking the case.

"Of course I remember."

"Well there's been a little change in the plan. The State isn't going to try to use the confession."

"What does that mean?"

"That means there will be a trial. Now they'll have to prove he did it."

"I'm not following you. I thought there was going to be a trial, all along, and that was why you would have to go to Troy."

"Bertha." He caught his impatience and took a deep breath. She might have wanted to be a lawyer, but she was not one. "Before, it was just about deciding how much time he would serve for a crime he confessed to. That decision would have been made privately, in the judge's chambers. Now the State can't use the confession, so there's the whole question of whether he did it. Charles told me it didn't happen the way she said. I think the confession was coerced."

"Why Foster!"

"Bertha, before you tear off on a tangent about how this case will destroy my law practice, you should know I can prove there was never any rape." He stopped and waited.

"Then he's innocent?"

"Yes." Foster was not quite as sure as he sounded. His client was innocent of violent, forcible rape: that much was clear from the examination by Dr. Stewart. Miss Elizabeth was not only intact; there were no signs of blood or bruising—though it could come down to how the law defined rape. "I'm certain he's innocent of what he is charged with."

"Why Foster, then I think you are noble to defend him!" She clasped his hand and squeezed. Her eyes widened and glistened.

Her reaction caught him off guard. She had originally urged him not to represent a confessed Negro rapist, even though it would have been done privately, in chambers, because the word would still get around and hurt his career. But now that he would be defending the same man in a very public trial that everyone in south Alabama would hear about, she was delighted, and simply taking his word, without more, that Charles was innocent, making it unnecessary to go into detail about the evidence of Miss Elizabeth's virginity, something he had been dreading having to do with her.

And she had called him noble. Her praise lifted his spirits, renewed his determination. For a moment, it was not only about his beloved Constitution; he also must not disappoint Bertha. Pulled by a tide of unaccustomed emotions, he decided to retreat to a neutral topic. "I always thought Troy was treated unfairly in the press and that our boll weevil monument was a little silly."

"And *I* think it is a delightful homage to the peanut!" Bertha said, still holding his hand.

Chapter 13

THE PROMINENCE of the peanut in my boyhood calls to mind a cherished Beck family document, a letter received by my grandfather, Mr. M. L., from Dr. George Washington Carver. I believe my father first showed the letter to my mother at or about the time he told her the case would be going to trial. I know that just before the trial, he was required to pay a visit to Mr. M. L., and my guess is that he would have shown my mother the letter as a way of explaining his father, a man she did not particularly care for and was a little intimidated by. Given that my mother's own father had named his firstborn son Abraham Lincoln and his second William Seward, along with his sympathy for the imprisoned Socialist Eugene Debs, I think my father wanted to show her the letter out of pride in his own family's progressive credentials.

"Speaking of the boll weevil statue and the peanut, there's something I've been meaning to show you, Bertha, if you will stop by my office for a minute. It's a letter to Daddy from Dr. George Washington Carver. You've heard of Dr. Carver at Tuskegee?"

"Of course, Foster. He's the colored man who figured out all the uses for the peanut. Everyone's heard of the wonderful Dr. Carver."

Foster knew that not everyone who had heard of Dr. Carver thought it was wonderful for a Negro to rise so high on his intellect, but he no longer wanted to argue and pick at Bertha; instead, he wanted to bask in her praise of him for sticking with Charles White while also subtly showing off his own family. "Well, Bertha," he said, still holding her hand, "all the talk about Dr. Carver caught Daddy's ear. He wanted to meet the man himself. Daddy used the occasion of having to fetch Frances from Eclectic—it was back when you two were teaching there before moving to Enterprise. He checked the road and figured he could go by Tuskegee and still get to Eclectic before night."

"You think Mr. M. L. just wanted to see for himself a really, really smart colored man?" Bertha teased.

"Daddy didn't go see Dr. Carver thinking he was going to see a curiosity," Foster said, releasing her hand. He wanted to explain his father to Bertha; he wanted her to respect him, even if she did not especially like him. "Daddy fancies himself as someone like Dr. Carver—an intellectual, but the useful kind." Foster opened the door to his office and held it for Bertha.

"Daddy likes to write articles and correspond with interesting people, colored or white, all over the country," Foster said. "I've been meaning to show you this letter. Daddy got it from Dr. Carver after he wrote an article about him in the *Troy Messenger*. Daddy lent me the letter and I keep it here in the office." Foster reached into a cubicle of his father's old rolltop desk, took out the letter, and handed it to Bertha.

Mr. M. L. Beck   *June 5, 1934*
Glenwood, Ala.

My dear Mr. Beck,

Your much appreciated greetings along with your write up in "The Troy Messenger" has just reached me.

In your beautiful and fascinating article it is difficult for me to realize that I am the subject of such a splendid article.

I wish I could live within hailing distance of the many lovely things you have said about me.

I am especially glad to get in touch with you, as I do not recall our having spent a more delightful, pleasant, and profitable hour, than with you.

I trust your young son will catch the rare dream of his parents, the only thing that will develop the mighty, undeveloped resources of the South and make it the richest section of the entire United States.

Please keep in mind, your promise to spend an entire day at Tuskegee.

Since meeting you, I have felt refreshed and more like making a strenuous effort to render better service in the future than in the past.

I am sincerely and greatfully yours.

                                                G. W. Carver

"What a wonderful letter!" Bertha exclaimed. The high school English teacher chose not to mention the misspelling of "gratefully" that had escaped Foster's notice.

"Daddy's proud of that letter."

"He should be."

"Daddy likes to see himself as set apart from ordinary men. Not just from the white trash—from the white gentry, too. There's not another man in Alabama with a letter like that."

Bertha did not reply. She was convinced there was not another man in Alabama like Mr. M. L., letter from Dr. Carver or no. She wondered if Foster was trying to match his father or do him better.

"Anyway," Foster said, "I need to go to Glenwood tomorrow to see Daddy. I'll be back the same day. Glenwood's not as far a drive as Troy."

Chapter 14

SOME OF MY HAPPIEST MEMORIES revolve around Glenwood, Alabama, and the handsome two-story home my grandfather had proudly built—from pine and hardwood trees grown on his own land, from lumber cut and planed at his own sawmill—for his adored wife and their five surviving children. During summer vacations, I would stay in Glenwood for weeks, riding the rural mail route in the mornings with my Uncle Charlie, who lived with my Aunt Elizabeth in a smaller home on an adjoining lot, fishing, and sometimes camping on the Conecuh at night.

Once school started we could visit only on weekends. My father and I drove from Montgomery to Glenwood about once a month. My first stop once there was always my grandfather's special room— a combination library and museum. I don't recall paying much attention to the books, because he had so many more interesting things to see: two enormous hornets' nests nearly the size of basketballs, a coffee can full of Creek Indian arrowheads, a Creek mallet, a tree root shaped like a snake to which someone had added beads for eyes and a carved smile, two deteriorating, tissue-thin Confederate dollars housed in a protective glass picture frame, a piece of petrified wood acquired on a trip to Texas, a miniature, perfectly formed iron anvil brought to America by an ancestor. A muzzle-loaded Confederate musket that children were forbidden to touch—because no one knew if it was still loaded and no one wanted to test it to find out—hung high above the hornets' nests. On a wooden placard, beneath the words "Trophies of the Years," the name "M. L. Beck" was spelled out in rattlesnake rattles.

After poking through the latest acquisitions, I would listen for a few minutes to the adults' conversation before heading to my grandfather's store, just three blocks from the house. Although my memories are from the late 1940s and early 1950s, the store and the town had not changed much from the time of the trial, just a few years earlier; besides, I have my father's handwritten description of the store in those days to supplement my memories.

The commercial center of Glenwood in 1938 was M. L. Beck General Merchandise, a two-story building of pockmarked red bricks and graying mortar. All kinds of goods could be purchased there. On the first floor there were barrels of sugar, flour, and dill pickles, gunny sacks of raw coffee and seeds, boxes of plug tobacco, snuff, crackers, and cheeses, slabs of sugar-cured bacon and salt pork. Farther back, customers could find chicken feed, nails, axes, steel traps, knives, guns, ammunition, fishing tackle, plough points and plough handles, harnesses, cedar chests and bedsteads, and, in the rear of the store, patent medicines and coffins.

Upstairs there were bolts of cloth, reels of thread, and books full of patterns for the latest in ladies' dresses, as well as ladies' hats, all manner of shoes, boots, and coats, and finished men's work clothes alongside men's Sunday best. A wide back door, two stories tall, opened onto a freight platform where the Central of Georgia railroad made its much anticipated stops three times a week, down from five times before the Depression.

At the front door, Miss Loventrice, a conscientious Methodist too frail for mission work, watched over the jars of stick candy, tended the cash register, and kept the books—though only Mr. M. L. could approve the credit furnished each year to the county's white and black farmers for the seed, groceries, and merchandise they and their families needed to carry them through the spring and summer, until the crops came in and they could settle up.

My memories of the store square with my father's written history, though he provides some additional details. After confirming that "We sold dry goods and ladies and gents furnishings, groceries and hardware," the family history records, "In the fall when farmers brought cotton to town they wanted a change from their diet of sow belly and syrup and craved salmon, dry salt mullet, kit fish and wedges of hook cheese. A meat box was purposely located near the water bucket and, after a drink of water, what was left in the dipper was thrown in the meat box to keep the salt meat moist so it would not lose weight."

As for credit for those who could not pay cash, Mr. M. L. "had a slogan printed on his wrapping paper, 'I have always thought well of credit used and not abused, for it is capital that never melts away.'"

Across the unpaved, sandy-brown square from M. L. Beck General Merchandise was the U.S. Post Office, festooned with colorful signs advertising brands of chewing tobacco and snuff, the candidacies of any Democrats running for office, and Buffalo Rock and Coca-Cola, along with weatherbeaten cardboard announcements of fish fries and church revivals. Next to the post office stood a row of tin-roofed, single-story wooden office buildings, one of which housed M. L. Beck Timber and Lumber Company. At one end of the square was another row of one-story wooden buildings, some painted white, some peeling white, some unpainted, offering the services and wares of a pharmacy and healer, a live bait store, a beauty parlor, a blacksmith, and the town's barbershop, owned by an ancient Negro named Friday who catered only to white men. A small grocery store at the end of the row struggled to compete with M. L. Beck General Merchandise by selling fresh sandwiches from the back door.

On the other end of the square, an artesian well, two hundred feet deep, its flow said to be neither diminished by drought nor increased by wet spells—the same well where my grandfather stood toe to toe with a rival sawmill owner over the freeing from peonage of Will Pickett—bubbled up crystal-clear drinking water through a white marble fountain equipped with three brass drinking fixtures that piped runoff into a horse trough. Mr. M. L. liked to point out in letters to his correspondents up North that the drinking fixtures were not segregated by race.

If much of Glenwood's commerce took place at M. L. Beck General Merchandise, the flowing well was its cultural and political center. My father remembered and wrote in his family history of the time when he was a boy and U.S. Senator Hugo Black came to Glenwood to campaign. After being introduced to the voters by Mr. M. L., and surrounded by white men (the women and Negroes standing respectfully in the back), Senator Black made a rousing speech in support of the New Deal. By 1938, though, Hugo Black was on the U.S. Supreme Court and a new man, Lister Hill, a Montgomery lawyer and graduate of Columbia University in New York, held Black's seat in the Senate. My father admired Senator Hill but doubted he would ever bother to campaign at the well in Glenwood; the town was losing population as young men and women moved to the cities. I was told, only half in jest, that if you wanted to know the population of Glenwood, all you had to do was to meet the 5 p.m. Central of Georgia on any Sunday, at the platform behind Mr. M. L.'s store, because the entire town would be there.

But if the town, by 1938, may have seemed smaller to my father, I am certain his daddy still loomed large the day of his visit, just a few days before the trial in Troy of Charles White.

Chapter 15

MY FATHER soon figured out why he had been summoned to Glenwood that day: to be told not to take the case of *State of Alabama v. Charles White, Alias.* When the case only concerned whether Charles would spend the rest of his life or twenty years in Kilby prison, Mr. M. L. had not taken much interest in it. But now, word was his son planned to argue the Negro's innocence to a jury.

Mr. M. L. began the conversation not by bringing up Charles White, but by talking about what he saw as the cause of the race problem in the South.

It went back to the loss of the war, not to slavery or the war itself. The victorious Yankees pompously called what followed the loss "Reconstruction," but it really was punishment, pure and simple. And that was what got the Klan started. Mr. M. L. was mostly repeating what he had been told by his own father, but, true to his nature, he claimed to have made an independent study of it, from which he had concluded that when it came to the causes of racial disharmony, the Yankees and Reconstruction were more to blame than Southern whites.

Have we made progress despite that burden, Mr. M. L. asked rhetorically, then answered his own question: of course we had. They were sitting on the porch of M. L. Beck Timber and Lumber, across the unpaved, sandy street from M. L. Beck General Merchandise. Mr. M. L. was doing the talking, except when he was interrupted to receive greetings as the town of Glenwood, colored and white, ambled back and forth across the square. For the moment, Foster thought, his father seemed to be his old self, a tall man for south Alabama, a physically domineering gift he used to full advantage. He was intellectually domineering as well, in the Alabama, Mississippi, Louisiana, and East Texas towns he had visited. While Mr. M. L. had never traveled up North, he had taken pleasure in corresponding over the years with newspaper editors in places like Philadelphia, Boston, and New York as well as with a rabbi in Chicago, and he claimed to have learned much about other parts of the country from those exchanges. His collection of books by Jack London, Stephen Crane, Charles Dickens, Shakespeare, Bret Harte, Herman Melville, Nathaniel Hawthorne, and Mark Twain, along with the wild animal stories of Ernest Thompson Seton, the *Encyclopedia Britannica*, and histories of the world by Ridpath and of the Jews by Josephus, spilled out of three tall mahogany cases.

Foster knew his father was right. There had been progress; he had heard about it for years and he would hear it again now: his father's routing of the Klan—it was why some Crenshaw County Negroes were alive; his freeing of Will Pickett from the chains of peonage; his payment and promotion of Tump Garner; his letter from Dr. George Washington Carver . . . which reminded him, he wanted to get that letter back so he could frame it and hang it in his library.

"Daddy, I know all that's the truth. But you said yourself it was also paternalistic."

For a moment Mr. M. L. seemed to be stumped, trying to remember if he had ever said any such a thing. But if he had said it, he assured his son, there was no harm in a little paternalism, in helping people when they couldn't do for themselves. Foster himself, he recalled, had been a sickly, coddled baby and was even now the puniest of his litter, boy or girl.

Mr. M. L. glowered behind bushy eyebrows and angrily rapped his pipe bowl against the side of his front porch rocking chair, shaking yesterday's tobacco remains into the sand that had been deposited a millennium ago, when parts of south Alabama lay beneath the Gulf of Mexico. During the centuries that followed, the pure white sand left behind by the receding Gulf waters had mixed with the black belt alluvium washed downstream by Alabama's mighty rivers, producing a fine-grained, beige-colored soil.

Foster knew there was no point arguing how it could be better, knew his father had more to say. In the silence, three crows mocked a newborn calf that wobbled to its feet in the green pasture behind the flowing well. A Negro man of indeterminate age whom Foster had seen from time to time over the years but did not know by name watered his mule at the trough. Two white men stood off to the side of the drinking fountain, under the shade of an ancient water oak, watching the Negro and his mule. The crows, their voices gradually becoming fainter, flew off to torment another animal. In the distance, Foster could hear the faint, familiar metal and wood sounds of a cotton wagon clattering across the Conecuh River wooden bridge nearly half a mile away, the loose planks rattling one by one.

Foster decided it was time to get to the point of the visit. "What if he's innocent, Daddy?"

Then he would get off. He wouldn't need Foster.

"No one in Enterprise will even know I have the case . . ."

His father said he knew. If it was known in Glenwood, it would be known in Enterprise.

Mr. M. L. stopped, smiled, and said good morning to two Negro women, who smiled back as they crossed the square, headed to M. L. Beck General Merchandise. They would buy their families' needs with M. L. Beck coins, not the Yankee dollar. "I didn't invest all that money in your education so you could throw it away on some Nigra from *Dee*-troit who had no business being in Troy to begin with," his father said, oblivious to whether the women were out of earshot.

"You raised all of us to be fair to Negroes, Daddy."

Mr. M. L. agreed with that, but said he didn't raise his children to stir up trouble when they didn't have to. Judge Parks could get the Negro a smart Yankee lawyer.

"Why not one of us, an Alabama lawyer?"

The answer came easily: because we live here.

"It comes down to this. Are we in Alabama a government of laws, not of men, like you always said we were?" Foster was remembering talks around the family dinner table when he was a boy. "After Scottsboro . . ."

His father didn't want to even hear the word "Scottsboro." He said his son didn't know what happened there.

"But they deserved to have a lawyer."

Mr. M. L. agreed with that. But it didn't have to be someone who lived in Scottsboro, and it wasn't. You push this thing too fast, you'll set us all back, he said. And the Negroes would be the ones who would suffer if race relations were set back.

Further analysis was interrupted by his father's violent fit of coughing, followed by repeated throat clearings and spitting into the sand. Foster waited, then finally said, "Daddy, you should ask a doctor about that cough. You really should."

Foster knew it was pointless to tell his father to ask a doctor what he should do about the cough. His father dismissed anyone who tried to tell him what he should do, especially if the "should-do" advice came from anyone in the medical profession. Mr. M. L. had already heard a lifetime of what he should do from his father-in-law, a former Confederate Army surgeon—a man, Mr. M. L. joked, who was responsible for more Confederate deaths than General Grant.

The coughing subsided. Mr. M. L.'s tone became softer, almost affectionate. Foster knew the shift signaled a change in tactics. Mr. M. L., everyone said, knew how to sell, and he was about to try a new approach. "I'm with you, son, on your Negro's right to an attorney. That's a fine idea. But it doesn't account for people. White people today remember what it was like during Reconstruction."

"They remember what they were told. There's hardly anyone here today who was alive during Reconstruction."

"Oral history is all we have. You won't read our side in the Yankee's history books, but during Reconstruction, with the Nigra in control, white women were afraid to come out of their homes. That's why you have to be especially careful defending a rape by a black of a white."

"Alleged rape. In fact there was never—"

"Now we have well-intentioned ideas, the presumption of innocence, noble ideas. I agree with the ideas. And then you have the way things are in the minds and hearts of the people. That's what you don't understand."

"I understand this much. People are drawn to a winner, and I'm going to win this, Daddy. I can prove as a matter of law there was no rape."

"Maybe as a matter of law, but you can't enforce a law that's crossways with what a jury will support." Mr. M. L. paused to refire his pipe. Foster looked at his watch and thought of saying what *he* believed about law, but instead he waited as clouds of pipe smoke filled the air on the porch around them, then drifted off into the square.

"You were too young to remember the Tick Dip Law that came on after the panic of 1914. That was a well-intentioned law."

"Yes sir, Daddy, but I've heard you tell about it."

"I'd gone a little into the cattle business, that was how I came to follow it, but I might have followed it anyhow because of what it teaches about human nature. The county said you had to bring your cattle once a year to one of the dipping tubs. Big concrete county tubs filled with creosote and kerosene. The county workers drove the cows one by one up a wooden ramp and whipped and pushed on 'em till they gave up and jumped in the tub. The cows fought and bellowed, but what ended the tick dip law was the cattlemen, not the cows. The cattlemen hated the damn law. They would come around at night and dynamite the tubs. The county would replace 'em and the cattlemen would blow 'em up again. The county would put out a guard at night and they would blow 'em up again. Now, the Tick Dip Law was a well-intentioned law, but the men who passed it didn't understand people."

"I'm going to do it, Daddy. I'm going to do it because I'm a lawyer."

"You're a wet-behind-the-ears lawyer." The tone shifted back to assaultive. "You never tried a case like this. You'll get your Negro electrocuted."

It was in fact Foster's biggest fear: that he would lose at trial and Charles would die because of his incompetence. His father had figured out his fear and was going to use it on him.

"You know why you'll lose that trial?"

The fact that his father was not trained in the law would not deter him in the slightest from opining, so there was no point in saying "Why?"

"It's not because the jurors hate the Nigra, and I don't want to ever hear of you making that as an excuse. Decent Southern white men don't hate Negroes. You'll lose because decent Southern white men don't like one of their own coming in pious and trying to change things overnight." Mr. M. L. put aside his pipe and strained to lift himself from his rocker. Foster did not remember him having had so much trouble getting up, but knew better than to offer a hand. Mr. M. L. gained his footing, turned around slowly, and lumbered into his office. He returned moments later with a bottle and an opaque coffee cup—to passers-by, he was just having coffee—and poured himself about three inches of Four Roses, not offering any to Foster.

"Daddy, I agree with all that but—"

His father waved him to silence, frowned, drained off an inch or more of his bourbon. "I've made a study of this. The whites, the good ones your age, are ashamed these days about slavery. But you see, they don't know how to make up for it without causing trouble. And they may be right to worry about what would happen if things changed too quick."

"They ought to be ashamed of slavery. But, Daddy—"

"The ones your age are just now figuring out their granddaddies fought on the wrong side of the War." Mr. M. L. hesitated for a moment to tilt and peer into his cup. "Our unique sin," he said.

Foster smiled at his father's sarcasm. "We learned in school the Yankees had slaves too."

"Foster." His father rarely called him by his given name, and when he did, it was usually because he was impatient about something. "At first, North and South alike thought it was fine and dandy to have slaves, everybody knows that. Then it changed." Mr. M. L. finished the last of the Four Roses, stared at the empty cup. "The Yankees let theirs go before the middle of the last century. The Southerners didn't, and these days their grandsons are a little bit embarrassed—they won't admit it, but I know this—not just because their grandfathers didn't figure it out as quick as the Yankees, but for fighting the War over it, then losing the damn War to boot. It would have been different if we'd won the War, then we could have freed the slaves on our own and felt good about it, but no, we lost the War and the pious Yankees freed the slaves."

"I have never before heard a single Southerner say any of that," Foster said. He respected his father but lost patience with him when he was drinking. The conversation, he thought, had gone far afield.

"You see, son," his father continued, "the weight of that shame is bearable so long as it's only the Negro and the Yankee doing the condemning. As for a Negro's condemnation, well, the Nigra in Alabama pretty much keeps quiet, but only so long as we take our foot off his neck gradually. An Alabama Negro allowed to stand tall too fast will want vengeance. We all know that, and I for one know it's understandable he would. I would too. But we can't have a race war either, so we have to change gradually."

Mr. M. L. paused to nod at two white men coming out of the post office. "As for the Yankee's condemnation, there's not any weight to a Yankee's condemnation, all hypocrisy and lies. Alabama Nigras learn all they need to know about the Yankee from their cousins who move up North. As for Alabama whites, most don't like the Yankee to begin with, and they're damn sure he would do the same as we've done if he lived in a county with a Nigra majority. So we don't pay the Yankee's condemnation any mind, and that includes a Yankee lawyer appointed for this kind of case. A Yankee lawyer might even win this case of yours because a jury won't pay his condemnation any mind. But that jury'll see you as one of their own, a white Southerner. Just who the hell do you think you are, coming to Troy, trying to change things too fast? That's how the jury'll see you and that's why you'll lose and send your Negro to the grave."

"Only I'm not condemning anybody, Daddy." Foster's patience was exhausted. He wanted to drive back to Enterprise before the sun went down. "I'm just defending a Negro who has a right to a lawyer. And he's an innocent Negro. And before it's over, Daddy, I'm going to prove it."

And so it went, his father bullying him, yet also, he suspected, envying him. And there were new emotions to sort out. Part of it was the two of them for the first time trying to compete; part of it was his father still trying to protect him.

Chapter 16

F AMED CIVIL RIGHTS LEADER John Lewis was born on a
farm a few miles outside of Troy in February 1940, barely a
year and a half after the trial of Charles White ended, and has
less than favorable memories of the town. In his magisterial memoir
Walking with the Wind, Congressman Lewis recalled wondering, as
a little boy, why his mother said, "You must be very, very careful not
to get out of line with a white person." By the time he was ready for
elementary school, however, he could see for himself why she warned
him, because "by then, I had been to Troy."

"The place looks today," Congressman Lewis wrote in 1998,
"much as it did back then. There's the town square . . . dominated
by its statue of a Civil War soldier. LEST WE FORGET reads the
inscription on the statue's base, beside a brass plate inscribed with
the names of dozens of Confederate dead."

"Troy was always a town that knew how to fight," Congressman
Lewis recalled. "The major form of entertainment on weekends was
outdoor, all-comers wrestling matches on the town square. When
it came time to send its sons off to fight for the South in the Civil
War, the boys from Troy went," returning years later, "beaten and

wounded, many of their best friends dead," but still refusing to surrender.

I don't dispute the description of Troy by Congressman Lewis, but merely point out the obvious—that his memories as an African American growing up there and those of my own family were so far apart that they might as well have been recalling different worlds. Troy was regarded by the Becks of Glenwood, privileged white people, as a pleasant, cultured place to visit, a town, in my grand-mother's view, well worth a train trip to shop for her own and her children's clothes. The predictably different perceptions by blacks and whites sadly illustrates one of the many gaps between the races that existed then, and that in some respects continues to this day—and not only in the Deep South.

Although there are differences in the dates reported by the Troy and Montgomery press, the prosecution of Charles White appears to have moved swiftly from arrest to indictment. According to the *Montgomery Advertiser*, "C. W. White, transient negro fortune teller," was indicted on June 24. The *Troy Messenger* places the indict-ment on June 22. While the *Advertiser* wrote that the crime occurred on June 8, when "the victim" was "lured" to the home of Mary Etta Gray, the *Troy Messenger* reported that the attack was on June 6.

There is no dispute, however about the date of the trial, which commenced with the summoning of jurors on Wednesday, July 13, 1938. As reported by the *Messenger*, "The negro was brought to Troy Wednesday morning by a seven-member detachment" from the Alabama Highway Patrol; these men were joined by additional officers stationed in Troy. According to the *Messenger*, there was "no outward display of proposed violence" that Wednesday after-noon during jury selection, but as a precaution, Charles White was escorted back to Kilby prison in Montgomery on Wednesday evening by the Alabama Highway Patrolmen.

Judge Parks was prudent to insist that Charles White be escorted to and from Montgomery and that the Alabama Highway Patrol be present during jury selection. There was high talk in the crowd surrounding the courthouse when the word got out that two Negroes had been called for jury service in compliance with the Scottsboro ruling. But the talk subsided and a cheer went up when it was reported that both Negroes had been struck by the State of Alabama.

Judge Parks finally succeeded in impaneling a jury of twelve white men—each of whom swore he could render a fair and impartial verdict in a black-on-white rape case. The judge ordered the jurors kept together for the evening "under the direction of Special Bailiff Henry Bower," the *Messenger* reported, so as to avoid any taint of outside influence. The precaution turned out to be a wise one. That night, darkness and liquor emboldened some of the rough element to slip the leash and prowl the streets of Troy, looking for stray Negroes to bully and assault.

Foster would stay at the best hotel in Troy thanks to Judge Parks, a hotel that featured an elegant dining room, a spacious lobby, and an electric elevator. White-coated Negro porters served sweet iced tea to well-dressed white ladies and gentlemen who relaxed in rocking chairs. Guests could peruse the *Troy Messenger* or the *Saturday Evening Post* beneath an electric chandelier. To save on the expense, Foster had planned to drive back to Enterprise after jury selection and return early the next morning for the trial, but Judge Parks had arranged a room for him, free of charge. The owner owed him a couple of favors, the judge said, and he was cashing one in. Foster did not protest.

The nice Troy hotel must have seemed to my father quite an upgrade from some of the places he and his mother, father, brothers, and sisters stayed when not at home in Glenwood. In our family history, he recalled that on one of those occasions, in 1915, Mr. M. L., "a great one for making trips," loaded up the family in their Model T and set out for Yellow River in Florida, an all-day trip of 125 miles. "R. J., a young Negro who had been up North a while and was supposed to be able to drive and cook was the chauffeur," according to the history, but R. J. "knew little about driving and less about cooking," and so the family got only about halfway to Florida before getting stuck in a sandbed. "Fortunately, we had been told to take along a shovel for such incidents and were able to dig out. We got stuck [again] in a sandy creek . . . about four miles from the destination on the banks of the river. Our bedding and tent were to come by freight to a nearby town, but after a week had not arrived. We slept in a logger's shack until we all got sick with dysentery and went back home." The history records that "My family made quite a few trips to Florida in the Ford, but my mother finally rebelled at the work and hardship of cooking and looking after five children in camping conditions."

If my father's Troy hotel was a far cry from that Florida logger's shack, it was not unlike some of the hotels where he and Mr. M. L. stayed years later, in better times, for example during a well-remembered and frequently described trip to East Texas. My father had come home from college, eager to spend a week on his beloved Choctawhatchee Bay, fishing and camping before taking a summer job. My grandfather had other plans.

"You need to see some of this country of ours, my boy," Mr. M. L. had informed Foster the first day he got home. "Mr. P. B. and I will be your guides."

And so, after Tump Garner gave the Dodge sedan (the successor to the Model T) a thorough inspection, the three of them set out on a sweat-soaked, dust-caking trip in the middle of the summer across the largely unpaved roads of southern Alabama, Mississippi, and Louisiana. Foster did the driving when he was not patching and pumping up the twenty-one flat tires they experienced on the trip. Mr. M. L., who rode shotgun, did the talking. And Mr. P. B.—who was invited because he read books and was a good listener—sat in the back, spitting black streams of tobacco that coated his side of the car.

The journey took more than twice as long as it should have because Mr. M. L. refused to buy more than three gallons of gas at a time and insisted on stopping at every filling station in Mississippi, Louisiana, and East Texas to discuss politics, the timber business, possible kinships, or just the weather. Always, Mr. M. L. took a suite in the finest hotel in whatever town the three of them reached by sunset, with beds for himself and Mr. P. B. and the whores they invited up.

But if the Troy hotel reminded my father of those grand hotels along the road to East Texas, the mood inside was different. During the trip to East Texas, the personable Mr. M. L. could always charm the concierge into finding him whiskey, sandwiches, tobacco, whores, whatever his needs and no matter the hour; but at the Troy hotel, the stern-looking young white clerk just glared when Foster Beck of Enterprise signed the guest register and did not wish him a pleasant stay, and the white maître d' ignored him when he asked what was included with the entrees. When finally he was directed to a poorly located table—the jurors were being fed separately in a private banquet hall—the other diners frowned and whispered as the word got around that this was "the lawyer for the nigger rapist of a local white girl." My father finished his supper alone, not staying for dessert even though it was included in the price, and removed to his room to study his case file, without a single fellow diner saying so much as "howdy" or even nodding in his direction.

Chapter 17

According to *One Hundred Fifty Years of Pike County History*, supplemented by photographs offered by the Troy Public Library, the core of the Pike County courthouse was constructed of brick in 1881, replacing the original wooden building. In 1898, large, brick rectangular wings were added to each corner and white stucco was affixed to the entire building. The new front entrance—at the time of the Charles White trial in 1938, as when it was constructed forty years earlier—featured three arched doors beneath a four-columned second-story portico. Tall windows were spaced evenly on each side and on both floors, and four clocks facing north, south, east, and west, along with a weather vane, were mounted on an open, eight-columned cupola. The courthouse sat in the middle of the town square, bordered by watering troughs and hitching posts for horses and parking spaces for the growing number of automobiles, and it dwarfed the shops on the square where farm tools, fresh meat, guns, and dry goods were sold.

Early on the morning of July 14, 1938, Charles White arrived back in Troy, escorted from Montgomery's Kilby prison, the newspapers reported, by fourteen members of the Alabama Highway Patrol. This group was met just outside of town by two more state patrolmen stationed in Troy, bringing the grand total to sixteen. Pike County Sheriff B. R. Reeves and two deputies drove out to meet the state officers, bringing chains that turned out to be unnecessary, as Charles White had been shackled ever since he was removed from his cell in Montgomery. Owing to the intervention of Judge Parks with the Patrol commandant in Montgomery, all sixteen of the patrolmen would remain at the courthouse throughout the trial to ensure perfect order.

By 8 a.m., more than two hundred white men—a mix of well-barbered Troy shop owners in short-sleeved shirts and sun-browned Pike County farmers wearing brogans and overalls—had surrounded the courthouse. Plumes of dry dust raised by their Model Ts and mule-drawn wagons hung in the air as the men milled about, quietly shaking hands, exchanging greetings, speaking in low tones. A knot of teenaged white boys, members of the high school football team, joked, jostled, and swapped licks until warned by a deputy sheriff. Three elderly Pike County Negro men, dressed in their Sunday suits, had come to the courthouse at the invitation of Judge Parks, and they stood together, outside but near the front doors.

At 8:30 a.m. on the dot, Sheriff Reeves threw open the doors, and close to half of the white men who had been waiting pushed into the courtroom, taking with them the free fans imprinted with information about local merchants that were handed out at the door, and quickly filled the benches. A teenaged white boy was assigned to stand in the back of the courtroom, pay close attention, and run out to report, as developments warranted, to more than one hundred white men who could not find a seat and would have to wait in the foyer or outside on the square. Through prearrangement by Judge Parks, the three elderly Negroes were ushered inside separately by Sheriff Reeves and directed to an area in the back where they could stand out of the way and observe. To everyone's relief, the Negroes politely declined the offer of chairs.

Next to make an entrance were a number of middle-aged white women, dressed in long, plain skirts, simple blouses, and floppy bonnets. The women entered as a group but quickly separated as they found the seats they had ordered their husbands to save for them. It was understood that the women would be permitted to stay for a while but might have to be excused should the testimony become inappropriate for their ears.

The Pike County courtroom of Judge Parks was now filled to capacity. By order of the judge, the tall windows on each side had been left fully raised throughout the night of July 13, in hopes that the evening air would cool the courtroom. While this measure had been effective to a point, it had let in a small owl and lots of gnats and other insects. The owl was chased out by Sheriff Reeves's deputies, but many of the insects would remain in the courtroom and torment those in attendance throughout the day. The open windows also gave some the impression that sitting on the windowsills would be permitted. Judge Parks had anticipated such an infraction and a deputy quickly dislodged the offenders, who were forced to watch through the windows from outside.

The mood abruptly tensed and hushed moments later as Court Reporter Clarence McCartha, the clerks, and the lawyers entered, the lawyers solemnly taking their places at their respective tables and commencing to rustle papers. Next came the twelve jurors, solemnly nodding, occasionally smiling to their friends and neighbors in the packed courtroom, but avoiding eye contact with the lawyers as they had been instructed to do by Judge Parks.

It was time for the defendant to be brought in. At Foster Beck's insistence, Charles White's face had been shaved and his hair neatly trimmed, and he had been loaned a set of civilian clothes before leaving Kilby prison, but there had been a question about whether he would have to wear his shackles in the courtroom. "As Blackstone wrote as long ago as 1769, in his *Commentaries on the Laws of England*," Foster had argued to Judge Parks in chambers, "unless there is a danger, a defendant must be brought to bar without irons or any manner of shackles. The State of Alabama has not shown there to be any danger."

Judge Parks agreed. The defendant would not wear shackles when in the presence of the jury. As a result, Charles White was able to walk in with only a deputy holding his arm and to make his way unassisted to his counsel's table.

"All rise," an assistant clerk commanded the moment Charles was seated. The assistant clerk had moved to Troy from Boston. Despite having lived in Alabama for ten years, he had retained a stentorian Boston accent, which gave a martial tone to the words "All rise," the signal for Judge W. L. Parks to enter the courtroom.

Chapter 18

JUDGE W. L. PARKS, by the evidence of his obituary, had not attended law school. That was not unusual in those days, when attorneys often simply apprenticed with practicing lawyers before taking the bar exam. I remember my father saying that Judge Parks had a reputation for being fair and that he "could have done worse," a comment that was like him, for he was not the kind of man to blame others.

My father believed that Judge Parks chose him, rather than a Yankee lawyer, to defend Charles White as a way of demonstrating Southern self-sufficiency. In addition to my father's growing reputation, Judge Parks also knew of my father's law partner, Mr. Yarbrough, and the fact that this much older civic and business leader placed confidence in my father would have been reassuring to Judge Parks. The advocacy of a respected, if on the young side, trial lawyer from Enterprise, the son of one of Alabama's progressives on race, along with the strict courtroom decorum that Judge Parks had promised to impose, would go far toward convincing skeptics that the trial of Charles White would be as fair as any colored man accused of raping a white woman could have gotten anywhere, even in New York.

Judge Parks gaveled the courtroom to silence and directed everyone to be seated. He did not say good morning, and his tone and demeanor were solemn as the indictment was read: "The Grand Jury of Pike County charge that Charles White, alias William White, alias Reeves White, whose Christian name is to the Grand Jury otherwise unknown, forcibly ravished Elizabeth Liger, a woman, against the peace and dignity of the State of Alabama."

What was said by Judge Parks as he turned to face the jury does not appear in the transcript, but based on what my father said and the way things are done in court, he would have explained that what he had just read was what the law called an indictment: a formal charge of a crime but not evidence of a crime. Pausing to allow the distinction to sink in to each of the twelve jurors, all of whom he knew personally or through their families, he told them to base their verdict on evidence alone. Another pause, and then there was a change in tone; no longer warm, his voice held a warning.

In a moment, he told the jury, you will hear the opening statements of Mr. E. C. Orme of Troy, representing the people of the State of Alabama, and then of Mr. Foster Beck of Enterprise, who will represent the accused, Charles White. What the lawyers say in these opening statements, Judge Parks explained, will not be evidence. It will only be what the lawyers *expect* the evidence will be. And that is all they would say, he warned, or he would put a halt to it. Judge Parks gave each attorney a stern look, as if to reinforce to one and all that this was his courtroom, not theirs, and that he would brook no impertinence, holding their eyes until each nodded his assent. The lawyers would not be permitted to tell the jury the law. Judge Parks would do that.

Turning from the lawyers to the packed courtroom, Judge Parks said that the Alabama Highway Patrolmen everyone had seen would deal with any disturbances by the crowd outside. There would be no talking, and no stirring or commotion, inside, or he would have the sheriff clear the courtroom of the offenders.

Judge Parks paused for emphasis before saying, "Sheriff Reeves?" Sheriff B. R. Reeves considered rising up from his chair beside Mr. McCartha but decided it was not worth the effort. Everyone knew who he was. The sheriff contented himself with pressing down on the arms of his chair and straining to lift his posterior an inch or two before collapsing back on the seat.

"BE IT REMEMBERED that on the 14th day of July, 1938, in the Circuit Court of Pike County, Alabama, Hon. W. L. Parks presiding, the following proceedings were held," Court Reporter McCartha recorded in shorthand, "ELIZABETH LIGER, a witness for the State, being first duly sworn to speak the truth, the whole truth, and nothing but the truth, testified as follows on Direct Examination."

"My name is Elizabeth Liger. They sometimes call me Cain Liger. I am twenty years old. I will be twenty-one this September 17."

As most people in Troy knew, Elizabeth "Cain" Liger was the daughter of the family that owned the Liger grocery store in town. Although one of her arms was deformed, Elizabeth Liger was otherwise of a modestly athletic build, with straight-line hips, long, slender legs and undeveloped breasts. She looked a little younger than twenty going on twenty-one, but sounded a little older when she spoke. Some in Troy had told Foster she was "slow"; others said no, she was just "dreamy," a "silly girl" who would be fine when she married and had some children. Everyone agreed she believed in fortune-tellers.

Solicitor Orme asked her if she knew Mary Etta Bray.

"I do know Etta. I have been knowing her about two years and have been seeing her all along."

Solicitor Orme asked how long she had known Charles White.

"The first time I saw him was in the store last month. That is him sitting over there."

"Indicating," Mr. McCartha recorded in shorthand.

"Miss Elizabeth," Solicitor Orme asked, "did Charles White do something to you?"

Foster tensed, but he did not object. The story was going to come in sooner or later; an objection to the leading question would look as if the defense was afraid for the jury to hear what had happened.

"Yes, Charles White did something to me. It was on a Tuesday down at Etta's house where he was staying. When I got down there, Etta showed me to Charles White's room."

"Did you ask to see Charles White?"

"I did not ask for Charlie. She knew what I wanted and she led me to the room. Mary Etta did not go in the room with me. It was just he and I in there. Then he locked the room."

"Please tell the jury what happened next."

"I told him I came to have my fortune told. He said it would be twelve dollars and he was going to fix me up."

"Miss Elizabeth, did anything else happen other than the fortune-telling?"

"After he got through telling my fortune he told me to come over to his side of the table where he was sitting. When I got over there he pulled up my dress and took some kind of salve and put it on me right down there . . ."

"Indicating," the transcript recorded.

"On my private parts."

"Did he do anything else to you that Tuesday?"

"He told me to get on the bed, he was going to fix me up, and I told him no he wasn't going to fix me up there on the bed, and he got on top of me then. He pulled up my clothes and pulled off one part of my shorts. I cried but it didn't do any good. I could feel something stinging down there—a stinging, and a funny and burning feeling down there, and I asked him to get off me but he would not do it, and every time I cried he put his hand over my mouth and he said, 'If you tell anybody I am going to kill you.' He was lying on top of me and he was just so big and fat he hurt me when he lay down on me."

The State then asked the following question: "Did you see him undo his clothes?"

The defendant objected to this question as leading, the transcript recorded, but there was no ruling by the court.

"Yes, I saw and know what a man's private parts are. Yes, I saw him do something about that. He got it out and then stuck it in mine. I couldn't tell how far because you see I was looking the other way when he got on top of me. All I could tell was just when he was putting it down there was it would sting and it would feel funny and burn. I wasn't in that position only about two or three minutes. That was about as long as I was on the bed. When I was on the bed his right arm was back of my neck. I think it was about that far . . ."

"Indicating," the transcript recorded.

"Around my neck if I am not mistaked.

"Whenever I asked him to get off, he wouldn't do it and he said he wanted to stay on there a little longer, that he wanted to get off. When he got off I got up. I put my shorts back on. I started to open the door. I didn't know it was locked and I couldn't get out and he pulled me back and he felt of my breasts and he said, 'When this boy meets you he is going to feel your breasts like that.' "

"Indicating," the reporter noted in shorthand.

"He said, when the right one comes to meet me this is what he will do. That he would feel my breasts, and he said that would make them big. And then he unlocked the door and he opened it and let me out. I started home then. I saw Mary Etta and her girl in the house. Mary Etta was in the kitchen, I think, fixing dinner. I told her about what he was doing to me. She said, 'He wasn't going to hurt you,' that 'he was as good as gold.' "

The defendant moved to strike what was said about Mary Etta. The court ruled that what had happened could be shown, but not the details of the conversation.

The witness continued: "I went on home from down there. When I got home I saw Mr. Scarbrough down at the store. I told Mr. Scarbrough when I went to the store."

"Nothing further," Solicitor Orme said, and returned to his seat.

Chapter 19

"MISS ELIZABETH," Foster Beck said on cross-examination, speaking softly. "I have just a few questions, if you please." He had thought long and hard about whether to cross-examine Elizabeth Liger at all, and if so how, but he had decided there was no choice. Something apparently had gone on between his client and the young white woman, but he did not think for one minute that it was rape. And he was curious about her mention of salve.

"You first went to see Charles White on a Monday, the day before what you just described, not on Tuesday, isn't that right, Miss Elizabeth?"

After some confusion about the days, Elizabeth Liger agreed that Monday was the first day she went to see Charles White. "He came to the store, he and that negro woman, Mary Etta. She called me out there on the front of the store and she told me he was a fortune-teller. She said, 'That man in there was the best fortune-teller that had ever been put out in the state and he guaranteed it, and I wanted you to come down there and let him tell yours.' And, of course, I said 'All right.' I went down there to see him Monday."

"You went alone?"

"I went by myself. I told him that I wanted to have three questions answered for a quarter. He said he could answer any three questions for a quarter. The first question was something about the right husband."

"He said you would have a husband?"

"Yes, by the Fourth of July. I think the next question was whether I was going to have a pretty home and pretty furniture, and was I going to be happy, something like that, but I don't remember what he said. I think the third question was to describe my husband and how he looked. He said he was tall and curly-headed and had black curly hair, and then I think after that, he told me to come over there a minute that he was going to fix me up."

"That was on Monday?"

"That was on Monday. He told me to come over there and he would put some of that salve and rub on it, and he said it was about closed up now. He said he was going to fix it so this boy when he come could open it and have more fun."

"And he rubbed salve on you that same day, that Monday?"

"Yes, he rubbed some salve on me then. That was the first time he rubbed any on me. He rubbed right down there—on my private parts. I stood up and he pulled up my dress and rubbed the salve on it. I was standing up. I had on my shorts then. He didn't pull them off then, he just got them down there on this side and just rubbed it on."

"On your private parts?"

"Yes, he got it up in there. I asked him what was that for. He said he was going to, you know, make it open wider."

"What did you say?"

"I didn't say anything. I stood there I reckon about a minute or two. When he got through rubbing that salve I pulled my dress down. I knew that he gave a full reading. I told him I was going to come back Tuesday and let him give me a full reading."

"And you said this after he put the salve on you?"

"That was after he had put the salve on me."

"How long were you with him that Monday?"

"I was in the room with Charles something like forty-five or fifty minutes or an hour. I didn't stay in there long after he rubbed the salve on me. I talked to him about a full reading. That was all I talked about."

"And then?"

"When I came out of the room I stood there and talked to Mary Etta a little bit. I reckon I talked about ten or fifteen minutes to her. After that I went back home. I went to the store. Mr. Mance Scarbrough and my brother, Harold, run the store. Mr. Scarbrough is a clerk there. I told Mr. Scarbrough about going down there and having this fortune told, and I told him about paying the quarter and getting the three questions answered."

"Did you tell him about the salve?"

"Yes, I told him about Charles rubbing the salve on me. I told him everything."

"Did you tell your brother?"

"I didn't tell anybody else about that, just Mr. Scarbrough."

"When did you next see Charles White?"

"It was about the same time the next day when I went down there—about 2:30."

"You brought him some money?"

"Yes, I had my dollar."

"And where did you get that dollar?"

"I got it at the store. Mr. Mance Scarbrough gave it to me after I told him what I was going to do with it."

This produced some chuckles and head-shaking in the audience; most people knew that Mance had never given away a dollar to anyone in his life.

"And then you went back to see Charles White with the dollar? Did he use any salve that time?"

"When he gave me the dollar reading he rubbed some salve on me. When he got through with the reading, he told me he was going to fix me up real good for twelve dollars. I told him that I wanted a husband and a home and two children, a boy and a girl, and that I didn't want my brother and my mother to be mad with me, and he said he could get that. I asked him how much he would charge and he told me it was twelve dollars. I told him I would go home and get what I had, that I didn't have but only ten dollars and he told me that would be all right and to bring the ten dollars and owe him two dollars, and after that I said to him, 'No, I haven't got but $8.65,' and he said, 'Well, that will do, just bring me what you have.' When I came back nobody showed me how to go in the room there . . ."

At this point, the transcript reflects that the witness began weeping, but the court instructed that the examination proceed.

"I don't remember how long I was in there the second time [on Tuesday]. When I gave him the $8.65 he did not [sic] take an eyewater dropper and make a cross on me. He took that and put it on my breasts."

"With an eye-dropper?"

"Yes, sir, with an eye-dropper. He said some kind of a prayer or something. Yes, this man got on top of me. That is all I know, what I told you a while ago."

"And you spoke with Mary Etta when you left?"

"When I left there I went out of the house the back way. I saw Mary Etta in the backyard at the washtub. I think another woman was in the house. I don't know. I wasn't talking to anybody but Mary Etta."

"You know Mary Etta's daughter, Carrie Louise. Did you speak to her?"

"I don't remember passing Carrie Louise. I saw Mary Etta. I told her he got on top of me and told her what he done to me. I told her that he had just told me I was going to have a husband and children and I was going to get a husband before the Fourth of July, but I don't remember what else I told her. I might have told Carrie Louise good-bye. I don't remember."

"Did you make a complaint to Etta or Carrie Louise?"

"I did not make any complaint to them."

"You were not crying then?" Foster hoped Elizabeth would confirm that she was not crying; Carrie Louise had told him that Miss Elizabeth was not crying, and he didn't want to have to put a teen-aged colored girl's word against a white's.

"I was not crying then. I cried after I told Mr. Scarbrough. I told Mr. Scarbrough that this man told me he was going to fix me up, that I was going to have a husband and two children, and I told about him rubbing the salve on me and putting me on the bed and getting on top of me and that was when he took the phone and called up Harold."

Foster then asked the witness the following question: "How did he tell you that he was going to fix you up? With a husband and home, didn't he, and that was what he meant, wasn't it?"

The State objected to this question and the court sustained the objection.

"You didn't talk to your brother about it at all?" Foster asked.

The State objected to this question but there was no ruling, and the witness answered, "No, sir."

The defense then asked, "Miss Elizabeth, I will ask you again if this isn't a fact that this negro was polite and courteous to you all the time that you were there?"

The State objected to this question and the court sustained the objection. Mr. McCartha recorded that the defendant reserved an exception to the ruling.

"You have anything else before we go to lunch, Foster?" Judge Parks asked.

Foster did not want to stand between the jury and lunch. "Let me think about it while we all have lunch, Judge, if I may. But I do want to reserve an exception to your last ruling . . ."

"Already noted. We'll resume at one o'clock sharp," Judge Parks announced, bringing down his gavel.

"All rise," sang out the assistant clerk in his signature Boston accent, and all stood respectfully, moved by the drama they had just witnessed.

Chapter 20

MY FATHER was a prudish man, so I am not surprised that he never said anything to me about a "salve." Most likely, he did not know anything about the alleged application until Elizabeth Liger took the stand. As a lawyer who has been surprised by what a witness said in a deposition or in court testimony, I can well imagine what transpired during the brief meeting my father was afforded with his client, before the two had separate lunches.

"I'm telling this jury my side, lawyer," Charles White announced to Foster the moment Sheriff Reeves left them alone. Out of the presence of the jury, he was once again manacled.

"Charles," Foster said, "I've already said I don't want you testifying, and I've explained why. That's all there is to it. We don't have time to argue over it. Now what's all this about salve?"

"*Shee-uh*. I didn't touch that girl."

"You didn't?"

"You think I'm crazy coming to a town full of crackers, rubbing salve on a white girl's pussy?" Charles rattled his chains at the absurdity.

Foster's head was spinning. He didn't quite believe nothing had happened involving salve, although what Charles White said made sense. He would have to have been crazy to do a thing like that in Troy. "Then how do you explain what she said about your rubbing her down there with salve?"

"It's not *my* job, lawyer, explainin' what this crazy white girl's doin' with the salve."

"What do you mean 'doing with the salve'? Was she doing it to herself?"

"*Shee-uh.*" Charles White grinned. It was the first time Foster remembered him grinning, although it was a grin of contempt. "They all put it on they selves and rub with their fingers till they get off. Don't you know about nothing?"

"So you're saying *she* put it on?"

"I'm sayin' I didn't touch her pussy with no salve."

Foster was becoming impatient. He was pretty sure Charles was not telling him everything that went on between him and Elizabeth Liger. It was just too strange for Elizabeth Liger to have made up such a story out of whole cloth, and Charles was not saying there was no salve, just being cagey about who did what to whom with it.

Did it matter who rubbed salve on Elizabeth Liger? Maybe, maybe not, though he was curious. "Did you see her do it? Are you telling me you watched her put salve on her private parts?"

"Time's up," Sheriff Reeves announced. "You boys have to kiss bye-bye." The sheriff grabbed the slack in the chain that bound Charles White's wrists and jerked, but Charles stayed put in his chair. "Get your ass up, boy!" Sheriff Reeves shouted, reaching with his free hand for the billy club on his belt. Charles still wouldn't get up, but he looked to his attorney—the first time Foster remembered

Charles doing so for help, not in contempt. It was a small thing, but it was something.

"Sheriff, don't you yank him again," Foster said, moving between the two larger men. Then, turning to his client, he said, "Go on with him, Charles. We'll talk more at the next recess."

FOSTER HAD less than half an hour to decide whether to continue his cross-examination of Elizabeth Liger. He was hesitant to challenge her further about being raped, only to have the jury hear her swear again how Charles had pulled up her clothes, how she cried but it didn't do any good. As for what she did say, Foster suspected he could make her admit she stole the money from her brother's store, though maybe it was better to let that rest. He'd heard the laughter when she'd said that Mance Scarbrough gave her money, so the jury knew she'd lied. In the mind of the jury, did that lie make her a liar about Charles White?

And what to ask about the salve? Elizabeth Liger had gone back on Tuesday, after the first application, for "a full reading." Why? Did she in fact go back for more salve and rubbing? Dr. Stewart's report of his examination, which the jury would see, said there were no signs of violence to her private parts. So she must have consented to whatever went on—although twelve white jurors would not want to hear that a local white woman consented to some kind of strange sexual activity with a Negro.

From a window of the second floor, Foster watched small knots of white men amble back to the courthouse. Many of them were returning from bounteous noonday dinners at their homes in town—dinners of vine-ripe tomatoes, fresh cantaloupes, barbecued ribs, fried chicken, icebox lemon pie—the kinds of big, heavy dinners their fathers and grandfathers used to require after a hard morning of farm work in the fields. These town-dwelling store clerks and office workers no longer needed all that food in the middle of the day, but the habit was strong, and besides, it all tasted so good. And so they would cling to their big noon dinners, maybe cutting back at supper. As for those from rural parts of the county who had come too far in their mule-drawn wagons to go home for dinner, they would have had their wives pack delicious, home-cooked meals of pork chops and hard-fried egg-and-bacon sandwiches. Others—men without wives—would have made do at a general store across from the courthouse, where they could purchase "white meat"—pork fat that was battered and fried—along with homemade biscuits, ribbon cane syrup, bottles of chocolate milk, Buffalo Rock sodas, moon pies. At least Foster's meal of cold hoecake, ham, and a slice of blackberry cobbler was free. The Negro porter at the hotel had said, with a conspiratorial wink, that it was "on the house."

The men were returning early for a seat, though it would be another fifteen minutes before the trial resumed. No surprise that the men wanted to watch; a rape trial was better than the circus that had already made its yearly visit to Troy. Though, when Foster thought about it, what was it they really wanted to watch? With the circus, there was some suspense; an acrobat might fall from a high wire, a lion might turn on the tamer. Was there any suspense about the fate of Charles White? Would anyone in the courtroom believe Charles was innocent?

Foster removed his pocket watch. He knew he had been at his best defending civil, not criminal, cases—fighting economic power in the cause of fairness. And he did not like sex cases, not even civil ones. He had gotten through the bastardy case without having to dwell on the boy's intercourse with the girl because the baby looked exactly like his paternal grandfather.

His only other encounter with sex and the law was the time he had served as executor of the last will and testament of a retired judge. The judge had unwisely kept indiscreet letters from a paramour, which Foster found when he inventoried the estate. He had decided that the letters should not be delivered to the bereaved widow. "Why add to her grief?" he said to Bertha. "I tore the letters into bits."

"But of course you did," Bertha said reassuringly. "You did the right thing."

"Even though, as executor, it was my duty under the law of Alabama to turn over all property to her as the sole heir?"

"I approve," he remembered her saying with her teasing smile, followed by a sincere hug.

His thoughts returned to Charles and Elizabeth: would even one of the jurors sanction any kind of sexual contact between the races? He recoiled from the image—salved, thrusting fingers, whether they were Charles's callused black ones or her soft pink-white ones. Surely it was not something to ask her about on cross-examination.

"Time," announced the assistant clerk in his steely Boston accent. At the same moment, Solicitor Ewell Orme confidently strode up and grinned. "You gon' fish some more or cut bait, son . . . 'scuse me, *Mister* Foster Campbell Beck?"

"You'll soon find out," Foster said, gathering his notes, his mind at last made up.

| Chapter 21

THE SALACIOUS TESTIMONY of Elizabeth Liger had stirred the blood of the white men waiting for the trial to resume; feelings were at a boil. Besides, many had eaten far too much dinner, and gluttony, indigestion, the July heat, and lawyer talk had left some in a bilious mood. A couple of fistfights had broken out over whether seats could be reserved. But it was too hot to fight for long; the stifling courtroom quickly again filled to capacity and was abuzz with anticipation when Foster opened the back door and entered, with Solicitor Orme a step behind.

The impatient humming momentarily fell silent, then resumed. It was just the lawyers.

Again, the humming subsided as the jury entered, but it returned in force a moment later, as a low growl, when Sheriff Reeves brought in Charles White and pushed him into his chair.

"All rise!" the assistant clerk shouted, and Judge Parks solemnly reentered his courtroom, the audience falling silent.

"Mr. Beck?" Judge Parks asked.

"We have no need to ask anything further of Miss Elizabeth,"

Foster announced, trying to sound more confident than he felt. Had he succeeded in raising a reasonable doubt? He stole a look at the jury. They looked disappointed that Elizabeth Liger would not be asked more about her encounter with Charles White.

It soon became apparent to Foster why the State's next witness was Dr. W. D. Sanders. The born-and-raised son of Pike County had practiced medicine for an astounding fifty-three years, "or a little more," as he acknowledged with a chuckle. In the course of his long career, he had cared for most of the jury's families. Foster knew that when it came his turn, he would have to cross-examine the town's leading citizen with respect.

"Yes, I know Elizabeth Liger. In a way, I might say I have known her all her life," Dr. Sanders testified in response to Solicitor Orme's opening question. "I made a mental examination of her. I don't remember the date but it was recently."

"Doctor, as a result of that examination, what would you say her mental—"

"Interrupted," recorded Mr. McCartha in shorthand. "Defendant objected."

Foster now understood what the State of Alabama was up to with Dr. Sanders. The State had anticipated he would defend Charles White on the ground that there was consent. So the State would try to show through medical testimony that Elizabeth Liger was not merely slow but mentally incapable of giving consent. "With respect," Foster said, "the question calls for expert testimony. There is no foundation. The good doctor has not been shown to have the training to give such an opinion."

There was no ruling by the court on the objection. The witness continued.

"Yes, I have an opinion of her mentality."

"Now as a result of that examination, what is your opinion as to her mentality, Doctor?"

The defendant again objected and the court sustained the objection. "You will have to show more than that, E. C.," Judge Parks ruled.

Dr. Sanders wrinkled his aged brow into a frown. It was not the first time in his long career that he had testified in court. He understood the rules of evidence; they were much easier than keeping up in medicine: no foundation had been established yet for his opinion.

Dr. Sanders saw no point in waiting for the State to frame a proper foundation question. "I haven't ever made a specialty of people with different mentalities but I have had the common experience of other men. I have never made a specialty of it. There are some proceedings which doctors use which are recognized by the medical profession as to certain examinations." From long years of practice, and without moving another muscle, Dr. Sanders cracked open his wrinkled mouth, arched out his shaking lower lip, and blew a stream of breath up and over the tip of his nose, to chase away a persistent gnat.

"Now, Doctor," Solicitor Orme said. "As a result of your examination of Elizabeth and your observation of her, taking all that into consideration, is she a person of average mentality or a person below average?"

Foster objected, and Judge Parks again sustained the objection. "You will have to have him show there was some affliction of the mind or some disease of the mind," Judge Parks said.

"I made some examination of her family history," Dr. Sanders said. "In my judgment, she suffered from a disease that might have affected her mind—a birth wound, an injury to the brain at birth. That is my opinion."

The State then asked the witness the following question: "Now, does that produce any effect upon the body or the mind, Doctor?"

The defense objected on multiple grounds, including lack of qualification to answer the question. Judge Parks said, "I think that is the only way I can get at it." The defense reserved an objection and the testimony continued.

"That was our opinion, that the injury was an injury to her brain. It arrested the development of her mental power. It causes what we call spastic paralysis."

"Now, Doctor," Solicitor Orme asked, "Taking the family history and your examination, physical and mental, that you put her through, what would you say her mentality was?"

Before Foster could object, the proceedings were interrupted by a dogfight just outside the open window. The audience chuckled and nodded appreciatively, grateful for a break in the tedium of lawyers and their peculiar ways of pursuing the truth. The fight abruptly ended.

"Your Honor," Foster objected. Then he paused, aware of a stir in the audience. The murmuring in the crowded, sweltering courtroom grew louder, and it sounded angry. One of the wives whose husbands had allowed her to remain in the courtroom, notwithstanding the risqué testimony of Elizabeth Liger, vigorously fanned herself to show her exasperation with the lawyer from Enterprise and his petty objections. Was preserving an appeal record, Foster wondered, worth annoying the jury? "With respect, your Honor, this witness has not been properly qualified by the State as an expert to give such an opinion. And the testimony called for would amount to impeachment or disqualification by the State of its own witness."

Judge Parks frowned and held up his hand to signal the court-room to silence; for a moment, he appeared to be reading something in a book. At last, Judge Parks said, "Overruled."

"And it is not proper for the State to put up Miss Elizabeth as a witness for the State to rely on," Foster continued to argue, "and then seek to show that her condition of mind was not such that it *could* be relied on."

"Overruled," Judge Parks said. The transcript reflects that the defendant reserved another exception.

"Dr. Sanders?" Solicitor Orme asked, without repeating the entire question.

"I say her mental development isn't more than ten or twelve years old. In other words, that she is a child."

The courtroom gasped audibly and Solicitor Orme, showing confidence, returned to his seat without even saying, "Thank you, Doctor." It was as if the prosecution believed the case was over.

"You have anything on cross-examination, Mr. Beck?" Judge Parks asked, then suddenly wheeled on his assistant clerk. "Wake up that peckerwood!"

The clerk found his feet, hurried over to the sleeping juror and shouted, right in his face, *"Wake up, sir!"* The juror, frightened by the strange Yankee accent, woke up and yelled, "Mama!" Finally having something to really laugh about, the audience relaxed a little as Judge Parks brought down his gavel and again restored order.

On cross-examination, Dr. Sanders said that his examination of the Liger family history went no further than her parents who were "normal." He admitted, "I am only a general practitioner of medicine. I studied mental diseases but did not make a specialty of it. My study of mental disease was incidental."

For the first time, the mood in the courtroom seemed to shift a little. The audience didn't mind a firm cross-examination; they just didn't want to have to put up with all those windy technical objections.

The next witness for the prosecution, Troy doctor C. C. Bowdoin, testified, like Dr. Sanders over repeated objections as to lack of qualification, that Elizabeth Liger's "mentality" was "subnormal . . . about an eight- or ten-year-old mind."

On cross-examination, however, Dr. Bowdoin admitted, "I have never made any personal examination of Miss Elizabeth." He believed he could nevertheless give an expert opinion of her mental development: "Just from my observation; she has been around to the house and I have talked with her."

Foster thought that, as with Dr. Sanders, the testimony was unpersuasive, and took heart from the murmurs in the audience and the skeptical looks exchanged among the jurors.

Chapter 22

MUCH OF THE TESTIMONY by the next witness called
by the prosecution, Mance Scarbrough, concerned Miss
Liger's interest in fortune-telling.

"If anybody mentions fortune-telling or marrying," Mance said,
"she is a maniac on that subject, if that is the right word to use—"

The record shows that the defendant objected to the word
"maniac" and that the objection was sustained.

The witness continued, "Having her fortune told and getting
married is practically all her main talk. I mean, she talks it constantly
and anybody that claims to be a fortune-teller could—"

The defendant objected and the objection was sustained.

The State then asked the following question: "Well, if there was
a fortune-teller in the neighborhood, would she make efforts to go
and see him?"

"No, sir, she doesn't make any effort to go; she goes," Mance Scarbrough testified, continuing when the objection was overruled, "I
have known her to go three times a week to my knowing . . . Outside
of this peculiarity of fortune-telling, getting married, and this paralysis of her right hand, I know that we have to watch Elizabeth about

the cash and all that sort of thing. She has no idea of the value of a dollar. She will go in the cash drawer and get whatever she wanted. She will tote it out and throw it away."

At this point it may have occurred to Mance Scarbrough that his employer—Elizabeth's brother—might not have wanted the whole county to know that his sister stole money from the cash drawer, for he added, "That, of course, is more or less amongst the family," as the audience chuckled and elbowed and winked.

On cross-examination, Mance Scarbrough acknowledged that Elizabeth Liger could read and write and he contradicted her testimony that she told him about seeing Charles White on Monday.

Two neighbors were called by the State and testified about Elizabeth Liger's persistent interest in fortune-telling, and a father and son who had been sitting on their porch on the day of the alleged rape said she looked like she was crying when she walked back from Mary Etta's.

A third doctor was then called by the prosecution. Troy doctor W. P. Stewart, a graduate of Tulane Medical School, was the doctor who physically examined Elizabeth Liger on the day of the incident. Following a series of questions and objections about the possible effect of partial paralysis on the development of the brain, Dr. Stewart testified over objection that in his opinion Elizabeth Liger's mental development was that of "about a ten-year-old child—maybe twelve—not over twelve." But it was his description of Miss Liger's private parts that held the attention of the courtroom.

"I was called to her house and I went there and examined her on the bed. With the help of her sisters we put her in the tub and gave her a douche. Upon examining her private parts on that occasion I found her hymen, commonly known as maidenhead, was very thick. That it had not been penetrated. It had not been broken."

On cross-examination, Dr. Stewart said, "No, I would not say that a person, a young lady who desired her fortune told, that it would indicate an abnormal mind." And he said, "I wouldn't say that a young lady who wanted to get married would necessarily indicate an abnormal mind either."

Then he testified, "Yes, I made a thorough investigation of her private parts. I didn't detect any injury whatever. The orifice just outside of the hymen, that is to say the vagina, has certain inner lips to it. They overlap the hymen. You have a labium major and the labium minor. There are two sets of those lips. They were not injured at all. I didn't detect any blood or other evidence of injury to those parts. I didn't see any bruises or detect any indication of violence on any part of her body."

It is likely that no one present in the courtroom that day ever forgot what they heard Dr. Stewart say, though some did not hear all of it. Wives were escorted out by their husbands with the words "hymen" and "vagina" ringing in their ears; and in truth, the testimony was almost too much for some of the men. Dr. Stewart had to step down from the witness stand to minister to an elderly gentleman who had closed his store after running out of white meat during the dinner break and had come to watch the trial, taking a seat vacated by a woman after an earlier recess. "He just needs air," Dr. Stewart announced professionally, adding to his credibility and authority. And no wonder, for all the air seemed to have been sucked from the room.

"Let's take a recess," Judge Parks said, rapping his gavel smartly.

"All rise," the assistant clerk directed as the dazed audience shook their heads in disbelief over what they had just heard. Once in the lobby, some husbands patted their wives' hands reassuringly while others muttered, "That's the damnedest thing I've ever . . ."

And, "Shucks, I might want that Enterprise boy to represent *me* . . ." And there was, for the first time, some head-scratching and skepticism about what might really have happened, and about how it all might turn out.

GIVEN DR. STEWART'S explosive testimony, Foster was hardly surprised when Judge Parks summoned counsel to chambers immediately after his cross-examination.

Judge Parks unbuttoned but did not remove his black robe, took a seat behind his glass-topped desk, clicked his manicured fingernails on the glass, and said it was high time to plead this thing out. He was looking at E. C. Orme, but it was Foster who answered.

"He says he's innocent, Judge. I'm not sure he'll let me enter a guilty plea, not even with a chance for parole—"

Solicitor Orme interrupted. It wouldn't do any good to seek Charles White's permission to enter a plea for a life sentence with a chance for parole. The State wanted the death penalty.

Judge Parks became impatient. He reminded Solicitor Orme of what the doctor had said. The men on the jury—at least one of them, and it would only take one—would conclude there was no way that a 250-pound black man got between the skinny legs of that girl without breaking her maidenhead. Judge Parks let the image hang in the air. He did not need to add what the jury of twelve white men would assume: that a black man that big would have a cock as thick as a corncob, as hard as a railroad stake. Did Solicitor Orme know Doc Stewart would say that when he sought the indictment?

Solicitor Orme said he knew, and that under the law any unconsented penetration was rape.

Judge Parks cut him off, said he knew the law, and again

drummed his nails on the glass desktop. He was worried about a hung jury. He did not want to try this case again.

Solicitor Orme argued that a life sentence was not good enough for the community. Judge Parks angrily said it was his job to decide whether a life sentence met the community's needs.

"If you'll let me see him," Foster said to Judge Parks, "I'll ask again if he will let me enter a plea in exchange for life with a chance of parole."

Judge Parks rose from his chair, fastened the buttons on his robe again, and summoned the authority of a trial judge. Then his tone softened. You talk to him, Foster, he said. Sheriff Reeves will find a place where you can counsel him to do this. Then, lowering his voice, he said that if Charles White would take a plea, the court would spare his life and leave him eligible for parole in ten years. He said there was no way all twelve of the jury would ever acquit, so there were only two things it could be. One, somebody was unsure about guilt and wouldn't budge. If so, the court would call it a hung jury and retry Charles White. And two, if they were not hung on guilt, then sooner or later, tonight or tomorrow morning, that jury would recommend the chair. Because once a jury made up its mind that a Negro the size of that one had raped a white girl, they would recommend the death penalty, and the court would have to go with that recommendation.

Judge Parks turned to face the closed door to his chambers and shouted to his assistant clerk, who had been stooping behind the door trying to eavesdrop through the keyhole. He wanted to know where Sheriff Reeves was holding Charles White.

The clerk said he believed he was in the colored cell, and went to check.

He's in the colored cell, Judge, the clerk confirmed a moment later, back with Sheriff B. R. Reeves in tow.

Sheriff Reeves said the only place he had to put Charles White was in the colored cell. He thought Mr. Enterprise wouldn't mind sitting with the other coloreds.

"I'll need privacy with Charles," Foster said.

Sheriff Reeves sucked in his breath. He said he would not put those other colored boys in the white cell, not even for a few minutes, while Mr. Enterprise met with *his* boy in private. Sheriff Reeves reminded Judge Parks that it was against the law of Alabama to mix races in a jail cell.

Judge Parks said he knew the law. He told Sheriff Reeves to bring Charles White into his chambers while he met with his lawyer.

The sheriff was worried. Charles White could jump out that window and run off; he would need to stay in the judge's office to restrain him.

Judge Parks said he doubted Charles would jump out with the leg irons the sheriff had put back on him after he was transferred from the presence of the jury to the colored cell, and he said he wouldn't get far if he did. You bring him in now, he ordered Sheriff Reeves, and then you can wait outside the door. The judge would wait outside too.

Judge Parks stood up to signal that the problem had been resolved.

Chapter 23

I KNOW MY FATHER wanted to find a way to spare Charles White from a sentence of execution in the electric chair. As a smart trial lawyer, he surely would have worried over what was likely to be the verdict—sooner or later, in this trial or at the likely retrial—of an all-white Pike County jury in a "she said, he said" black-on-white rape case.

My research in the course of writing this confirms that he had reason to worry. According to a 2010 article in the *American Interest*, "The South put blacks to death far more often than whites—especially when the victim was a white woman. Of the 455 men executed for rape in the United States between 1930 and 1967, 90 percent were African Americans." An amicus brief filed in the Supreme Court by the ACLU of Louisiana and the NAACP Legal Defense and Education Fund cited statistics showing that blacks convicted of rape were more than six times as likely as whites to be sentenced to death. A tabulation by Death Penalty USA of Alabama executions from 1926 to 1965 for rape (excluding a handful for "murder-rape") reports that of the twenty-eight men either hanged or electrocuted, all but two were black (the two whites were described as "asylum escapees").

"The Court will give you a life sentence in exchange for a guilty plea," Foster told Charles in Judge Parks's chambers. "And you'll be eligible for parole, maybe in just a few years. Charles, I strongly recommend you do this."

Charles White, who had taken the judge's swivel chair unbidden, swung his legs up and propped his chained feet on the edge of the glass desktop. Foster thought this was ill-mannered, and worried the chains would scratch the glass.

"That doctor said she's a virgin," Charles mused. "How come she can be a virgin and be raped?"

"The law doesn't require all that much penetration," Foster explained. The subject was distasteful, but he owed his client the advice. "They can convict you for rape based on what she said happened and on the doctors' testimony that she was mentally a twelve-year-old—too young to consent. And keep in mind that Dr. Stewart did say there could have been some penetration—a half-inch or so—without breaking her maidenhead. And if the jury convicts, they will recommend the electric chair."

"Sounds like the judge, though, might not be inclined that way?"

The question struck Foster as interesting. Would Judge Parks give Charles life if a unanimous Pike County jury came back for death? Not if he wanted to be reelected next term. Foster glanced at his notes. Judge Parks had told him a few minutes ago that if the jury found Charles guilty and recommended electrocution, he would "have to go with that." Was Judge Parks serious, or just trying to bluff him into convincing Charles to plead guilty?

"Charles, I honestly don't know what Judge Parks would do if we don't enter a plea and the jury found you guilty and recommended death." Foster was struggling with how to put what he needed to say. "I think there's maybe a small chance he would not follow the jury recommendation, give you a life sentence, but then it likely would be without parole."

"Why don't I take my chances? When I testify, the jury just might believe me."

For the first time, Foster saw weakness in his client's eyes. Charles White did not look like he really believed that the twelve white men on the jury would take his word over Elizabeth Liger's and the medical opinions and acquit him.

"I think the jury should believe you, Charles, but we both know they probably won't. Besides, I have said you could not testify."

"What you gonna do? Tell me to sit down and shut up? You have to put a gag in my mouth, lawyer." Charles White swung his shackled feet down from the glass desktop and struggled to stand up.

"Charles, sit back down." The two men glared at each other, the black towering over the white. "Please," Foster mustered.

Charles White sat back down. "I'm gon' say my piece on the stand."

"Please consider taking a plea. You might get paroled soon. At least you'll be alive."

"Not how I want to live," Charles White said, almost in a whisper.

Chapter 24

MY FATHER WAS NOTHING if not thorough, so I am not surprised that he did not rely on Charles White having told him that he had no prior convictions. And he understood the likely effect on the jury if it heard about Charles White's prior convictions—crimes the jury would only know of if Charles testified.

"Have you been in trouble with the law before?" Foster asked. They were still in Judge Parks's chambers.

"I told you before, no."

"And you didn't tell me the truth. I looked it up."

For a change, Charles smiled at his lawyer without contempt. "You did that?" He seemed surprised, even pleased, that his lawyer had made that much effort on his behalf. He did not seem the least bit offended that his lawyer had not believed him.

"E. C. will know about your record too, and he'll use it if you testify. But he can't even mention it if you don't testify. That's another reason I don't want you taking the stand."

"You sayin' the jury will only know about my record if I testify?"

"That's right. E. C. can't bring up your prior convictions as part of his rape case. If he did, it would prejudice your right to a fair trial on the rape charge because the jury would think, 'He broke the law before, that means he probably broke it this time too.' To convict you for rape in a fair trial, the State has to prove this crime, not that you have a bad character. But once you testify, you're putting your credibility on the line, and then the State can use prior convictions—of what the law calls a 'crime of moral turpitude'—to challenge your truthfulness. And your past crimes are crimes of moral turpitude, take my word for that."

"Makes no sense."

"I know."

"Because there's that same—what you call 'prejudice'—even if I don't testify," Charles said, determined to puzzle it out on his own. "The jury, they think, 'that nigger must be guilty, else he would stand up and say his piece under oath.' Either way, I testify, I don't testify, they gonna say I'm guilty. *Shee-uh.*" Charles rolled his eyes to the ceiling, exactly as he had done when Foster first met with him at Kilby prison, swiveled in Judge Parks's chair, and silently stared at the glass-framed portrait of a man in Confederate uniform. The only sound came from the open window, someone outside repeatedly turning the crank of a Model T automobile.

Finally, Foster said, "Charles, if you testify, I'll need to ask you myself on direct about your getting in trouble before. Otherwise, they'll bring the convictions up on cross-examination and it will look like we were trying to hide them."

Charles swiveled back around and looked his lawyer in the eye. "You see, Mr. Beck, you have all this logic on your side, and I understand it might work in your world. But not in mine. Sometimes, I have to gamble. Now, I figure I have three shots in ten that at least one of them twelve crackers will have what y'all call 'reasonable doubt' after they hear me testify. But that won't happen if they see me scared to take the stand. There's no odds in that."

"You have the right not to take the stand. That's in the Constitution. I'll get an instruction to the jury that you have that right."

"*Shee-uh*," was all Charles said, his grin again contemptuous.

Foster waited, believing his client had more to say. Outside, the Model T owner shouted an oath, then gave up and retreated to a shade tree. A mule-drawn cotton wagon could be heard as it rattled by on the way to the gin.

"Now, Mr. Beck, if you ask me when I take the stand if I ever had trouble with the law, I'll swear, no sir, I have not. Cause the way I see it, there's a five in ten chance this solicitor's been too cocky all along to bother looking up my record. If I'm right, I'll slip by. So, if *you* ask me if I have a record, I'll lie. You told me not to lie, so don't *make* me do it—"

Charles was interrupted by a loud knock on the door. Sheriff Reeves, cracking the door, wanted to know if they were about finished.

"Hell's bells, Sheriff," Foster exploded. "I'm talking to my client on Judge Parks's order." Though the reason for talking no longer existed: Charles was not going to plead guilty in exchange for a life sentence and parole. Worse, he insisted on testifying. Foster couldn't stuff a gag in his mouth. And if he asked Charles on direct about other crimes—to mitigate the effect of having the prior convictions come out only on cross-examination—Charles would perjure himself, taking the remote chance that E. C. Orme had not done his homework, almost certainly to be shown, on cross-examination, that

E. C. had indeed done his homework, thus revealing Charles White, Alias, to be a repeat felon who had been lying when he said under oath that he had no prior convictions. In short, Foster realized—and without having the time to think through the ethical issues—he couldn't ask Charles to explain the prior convictions on direct since Charles would commit perjury, then almost certainly be impeached on cross-examination. And he couldn't keep Charles from testifying. Charles White had boxed him in.

"I'll tell you when I'm finished, Sheriff," Foster shouted, more in frustration with his client than in anger with Sheriff Reeves. "Don't interrupt me again, you hear?"

Foster turned his attention back to his client. It was Bertha who had suggested, in her roundabout way, that he should try to get to know Charles if he was going to represent him. He had dismissed the idea at the time, without trying to explain to her that it was the law and the facts that were important. Besides, he was not sure if it was possible for him to know Charles White. The man did not fit the model of any Negro he had grown up with: not the smart ones, not the sassy ones, not the ones who went to church, not the ones who didn't.

"I want to say it one more time, Charles. If we haven't disclosed the prior convictions on direct—and he will know about them, I guarantee you—he will make it look on cross-examination as if we were hiding them. Take the plea. It can make the difference between eventually getting out of this mess on parole and going to the electric chair."

Charles stared through him, expressionless. He was not budging.

Foster struggled with himself. He wasn't sure his client trusted him. Maybe that was why he was not following his advice. "Charles, you don't know anything about me." He paused, hesitating to say it. "Anything about my family, my daddy—"

"I know some. Couple of colored boys at Kilby told me what they'd heard. I'm not sorry you're my lawyer."

For the first time, Foster felt a little respect coming from Charles. He was ashamed to admit it, but the fact was, he had not thought much before about wanting respect from a Negro. Charles White had taught him to want that.

"If you are sure you want to testify—and you don't have to, under our Constitution—"

"I'm sure."

"All right. Whatever you're going to say under oath, you should go ahead and say it all to me now so I can try to break you down, like E. C. will try to do on cross-examination."

"I understand. I'll do that."

Chapter 25

AFTER CONSIDERING whom to call first for the defense, and still hopeful that Charles would not insist on taking the stand, Foster settled on Carrie Louise Bray, the daughter of Mary Etta Bray. Carrie Louise had a reputation as a reliable girl who could be counted on to fetch a white woman's wash on Tuesday and return every garment the next day, clean, dry from the sun, and neatly folded. She was washing clothes in her backyard on the Tuesday in question.

"Miss Elizabeth, she stopped and spoke to me before she went in through the back door," Carrie Louise testified. "When she left she come around by the washtub and told me good-bye. She didn't complain about a thing and she wasn't crying. I did not see anything apparently wrong with her." A second witness, Annie McCray, who was present at Etta's home on the day in question and was in the yard helping Carrie Louise with the washing, also swore that when the "young lady" came out of the house to leave, "she just said bye to Carrie Louise and went on up the street. She was not crying."

"Anything further, Mr. Beck?" Judge Parks asked wearily. He

did not expect the defense had anything more. He was furious that Foster had been unable to persuade his client to do what His Honor thought best. He did not believe there was a chance in a million the jury would unanimously acquit, which meant a hung jury and a retrial. And he certainly did not think Foster would put Charles White himself on the stand to testify. In anticipation that the defense would rest, Judge Parks had at the ready a Supreme Court-approved admonition to the jury that a defendant had the constitutional right not to testify.

Nor did Solicitor E. C. Orme think the lawyer from Enterprise would dare subject Charles White to cross-examination. Orme wasn't even paying much attention to the colloquy between the judge and defense counsel and was marking up his closing argument.

Foster rose. He had planned to ask for a ten-minute recess, one last chance to talk Charles White out of taking the stand, also to answer any last-minute questions if he were still determined to go ahead. But before Foster could speak, Charles White was on his feet.

"I want to testify, Judge Parks. I want to tell what did happen."

The angry stir that immediately began in the courtroom was mounting in volume when Judge Parks rapped his gavel—though not before the white boy standing in the back who had been designated to run outside and tell the crowd surrounding the courthouse when there was something to report—had bolted for the door. "The nigger's takin' the stand! The nigger's gon' *testify!*" the boy shouted to the crowd outside.

"We'll have perfect order here or I'll clear this courtroom this minute," Judge Parks shouted as he stood and pounded a mahogany gavel the size of a ball-peen hammer. "Sheriff Reeves?"

Anyone who had ever been arrested by Sheriff B. R. Reeves did not want to have that experience again, so the buzz in the courtroom quickly subsided.

Outside, the captain of the Alabama Highway Patrol detachment, seeing the crowd surge upon the announcement that Charles White would testify, ordered his squad to form a line and assume the position of "present arms." The advancing rabble held up, quieted down, and became sullen, convinced from previous unhappy encounters with law enforcement that the armed men from Montgomery might just as soon shoot them as not if they rushed the door.

Inside, the clerk asked Charles White if he would swear to tell the truth, the whole truth and nothing but the truth, so help him God. Charles White said he would.

MY FATHER TOLD ME that Charles White spoke in a tone and with a demeanor he had not previously seen. Because Solicitor E. C. Orme had been sternly warned by Judge Parks, in a whispered bench conference, that he had better not object to Foster's questions absent indisputable cause, Charles White's testimony proceeded without interruption, and is reproduced here at nearly its full length, as recorded by Court Reporter McCartha.

"My name is Charles White, C. W. White, William White. I am living mostly now in Ohio. My occupation is a cook and molder. I last came to Troy the first day of June, Wednesday morning, at the dawn of day. I stopped here as a healer and adviser. I stopped at Mary Etta Bray's house early that morning and I blowed my horn and I got no reply and then I went to Claire Cardwell's and after I went to Claire Cardwell's I came back to Mary's house. I set up my office in what I call the end room adjoining the front room at Mary Etta's house."

After testifying that he saw but never spoke to "the white lady" the previous week at the Liger store, where he had gone with Mary Etta "to get something in order to live on," Charles recalled seeing her again at the Liger store on Monday morning, the same morning Mary Etta told Miss Elizabeth that he was a fortune-teller. He said he was there looking for spare ribs and neck bones. "I didn't say anything to the young lady. She never parted her lips to me.

"The next time I saw her was on Monday evening. It was at Mary Etta's house. Mary come to me and said, 'There is a lady from the store that is here and she wants you to give her a reading and she said she has only a quarter.' And I said, 'I don't read for a quarter. I will answer three questions for a quarter but my reading is a dollar.' And she goes back and tells the white lady, and then in a few minutes Mary came back again and she said, 'She has decided to take three questions, must I bring her in?' And I said, 'If you like.'

"When she came in she spoke first, she said 'Howdy do,' I told her howdy and she says to me, she says, 'I guess I will take three questions for a quarter.'

"She took a seat and turned around a little bit and then she went to proceeding with her questions. Her first question was, 'I want to know is I ever going to have a husband?' And I told her, 'Yes, ma'am; in the near future,' and the next question was 'Can you describe him to me?' And I said, 'Yes, ma'am. He is three or four years older than you; he is fair-skinned, blue eyes and blond hair;' and the next question she asked me was, 'Would my people be mad with me if I got married?' I said, 'No, your mother might shed a few tears, but when she finds out that you have a good husband, her heart will shout for joy.'

"I had answered her three questions and then she got to talking about some boys out at a baseball park here some place. When she was talking about her people being cruel to her I said, 'I don't think that your people are cruel to you, but if you wait until you get older you will thank your mother for being what you call tight today.' When she said she had a notion to run away I told her not to do that.

"I didn't put any salve on her that day. I didn't put my hand on her. Nothing else happened, only she just talked. She didn't say anything about coming back but she did say this, she said, 'I want a reading,' but she didn't say when she would be back.

"She come back the next day, that is June 7. It was one o'clock when she came in. I was out on the front porch.

"The first thing that called my attention to her was that Mary came out on the porch and said, 'The store lady is down here again and she wants a full reading.' I was sitting there talking to Mary's brother and some other negro man on the porch and I had about forgotten about what Mary told me about the white lady. I opened the screen door and went in the hall and into my room and I hadn't hardly got in there until Mary and the white lady came and I sat down and she was setting in the same chair that she did before. The white lady sat still and I reached out and pulled the door to."

"Did you lock it?" Foster asked.

"No, I didn't lock it. There wasn't even any key there to lock it with.

"The young lady then said, 'I have come after my full reading and I want you to tell me everything and I have got my dollar for you.' I told her to shuffle the cards and she did and laid them down and I told her to cut them to her right and she cut the cards to her right, and I said, 'You must have been a fast pinochle player, or whist player,' and I said, 'Would you mind turning out a card on the first pile?'"

Charles's testimony proceeded, card by card, until finally the nine of spades was turned. "And I looked dead in her face and I said, 'The nine of spades says there is trouble here,' and she said, 'For me?' And I said, 'Trouble means between you and your people.'

"After I got through reading for her she asked me plainly, is there any more work that you can do, and what do you charge for it?' And I said, 'It all depends on what you want me to do?' And she turned herself out from under the table again and she said, 'I want a nice home and a good husband and I want children, and I don't want to live in this durned place'—that was what she said. I said, 'Well, it will cost you twelve dollars.' She put her hand on the back of the chair she was sitting in and she said, 'I haven't got twelve dollars; I have got ten dollars,' and I said, 'It will be all right; you can owe me the other.' And then she said, 'I haven't got the ten dollars; I have got $8.65,' and I said, 'Whatever you care to leave will be all right.' Then she turned around to me and she says, 'I will have to get it from my mother's book.' Then I said to her, looking up from where I sat, 'Are you going to steal from your mother?' And she said, 'No, it is money I have saved, my money.' And I said, 'Don't take money from your mother,' and she said, 'I will be back in a few minutes.'

"She was back in about ten minutes. I was in the room writing a letter when she came back. She came on in with a long smile on her face and sat down, and she ran her fingers in her bitty pocketbook, and she commenced taking out the money and the first bill she put down was a five-dollar bill and she had a one-dollar bill on top of it and she placed another one on that; she put down two case quarters, two case halves, one dime, and one five-cent piece. $8.65.

"Then I said, 'Now, you told me you wanted a husband, you said you wanted a nice home, a nice husband, babies, and you didn't want to live here.' I said, 'Would you mind raising and coming around here and face me?' And she got up and got in front of me. I turned and with my right hand I got a vial—it is a secret, holy oil that I get from India—and I said, 'I am fixing to use this; it is a process from India.' I had a new eye-water dropper that I got here in this city from a drugstore, and I made a sign below her waist outside of her clothes; I set that down and got another vial the same size which was load-stone perfume—you can't get it at any drugstore—and I made a sign from the left up on her chest and I said, 'I have finished; you may sit down,' and she went over and seated herself in the chair nicely, and commenced talking to me, and she said, 'When will I meet this man?' I said, 'The fellow that you will meet, he will treat you—' and then she cut me off, she said, 'Would he ask too much of me like the other fellow did?' I said, 'No, ma'am; you are going to tell him about all your troubles and he is going to act nice with you; he is going to marry you,' and then she says to me, 'I am going to the ball game Thursday,' and she said, 'Do you think any of those boys will talk to me?' And she said, 'If they do, I am coming back down here Friday and tell you.'

"That is all that happened down there. I never did lock the door. I did not put any salve on her private parts. I didn't even put my hands on the white lady. I didn't put her down on the bed. The lady treated me nice; she made me no advances at all. I treated her white. I wasn't ever scared while she was in there. The lady left at two o'clock. One officer came to the house and it was fifteen or twenty minutes to four. There was another officer came there and he asked me, 'What is the matter, boy?' And I said 'Officer, I don't know,' and then this officer said 'Come on.'"

E. C. Orme must have known he was not going to shake Charles White on the details. But Charles lost his gamble, because, as Foster had predicted, the State had obtained documents reporting the prior offenses.

"Yes, I was convicted in Michigan in 1917 for armed robbery. Yes, in January 1924, I was convicted at Springfield, Ohio, for the offense of burglary in an inhabited dwelling and got from twenty to thirty years. I [served] eight years and they turned me loose. I got to be a spiritual adviser and healer. It came to me when I was in prison."

As for the allegedly locked door, Charles steadfastly swore he didn't have a key to the room and had never even seen a key to the house.

Painful as it was for Foster to watch the prior convictions come out, it was better than if he had asked and Charles White had lied to him on direct, and then been shown on cross-examination to have perjured himself. His property crimes were serious, but he had never been convicted of rape, so maybe the jury would focus on the lack of evidence of *this* alleged crime? And Foster thought Charles's explanation of how he came to be a spiritual advisor and healer, "It came on me when I was in prison," might have gone over well with a jury that believed in forgiveness.

Chapter 26

THOUGH I WISH that before my father's death I'd been more curious about the Charles White case, I was at least interested enough to ask him about his closing argument to the jury. I was a young lawyer myself by then, and closing arguments are something young lawyers tend to focus on, if only because they have been repeatedly dramatized in books and movies—one of the most eloquent, of course, being the closing argument in which Atticus Finch urges the jury, "In the name of God, do your duty."

My father's closing argument was not recorded in the transcript. As a result, I have nothing but my memory of what he said to me and my knowledge of my father's lifelong, passionate belief that the law was there for the poor as well as the rich, for blacks as well as whites.

His was a jury of the humble: from my comparison of the fifty-five names and occupations on the jury summons with the names of the twelve who served (as reported by the *Messenger*), there were nine farmers, one dairyman, a store clerk, and a mechanic. My father knew, from asking them on voir dire, that these struggling working-class men, personally or through their kin, had suffered foreclosures, evictions, arrests, and beatings—or worse—at the hands of mean sheriffs and bullying prosecutors; their white skin had not shielded them from abuse. Here, he would argue, those same authorities had charged forcible rape where, plainly, there had been no such thing, and they should not be allowed to get away with it. In a free society, the law was there to restrain the government, not just to punish the poor man. Before the authorities—beginning with the sheriff banging, uninvited, on the door of the home at midnight, followed by the rough and humiliating handcuffing in the presence of wife and children, the jailhouse threats and interrogation, the days and nights behind bars without bail—before the State of Alabama, with all of its heavy, creaking prosecutorial machinery, could do all that to a man and then deprive him of his actual life, it had to prove, beyond a reasonable doubt, guilt of the crime being charged: forcible rape. And that was as true for a poor man accused of a crime as for a rich one.

It is easy to see the parallels between the populist closing argument I believe my father made to his jury and the fictional one. Atticus Finch told his jury there was "one human institution that makes a pauper the equal of a Rockefeller." On the other hand, no such comparison can be drawn between what the real and fictional judges said to their respective juries about the law that they should apply in a rape case. This is because Harper Lee did not write any instructions by her fictional Judge Taylor to his fictional jury. However, I have the transcript of exactly what Judge Parks told the real jury in *State of Alabama v. Charles White, Alias*, and it is worth quoting as it illuminates, if it does not justify, what was to come.

"Rape," Judge Parks explained, means the defendant "forcibly had sexual intercourse with Elizabeth Liger." Before discussing the meaning of the word "forcibly" and the concept of consent, the Judge said, "First, I will say the sexual intercourse is complete under the law if there was any penetration of the vagina. [A]n emission on the part of the male . . . is not, under our present law, necessary."

Thinking, I suspect, of the extraordinary testimony by Dr. Stewart that Elizabeth Liger was intact following the alleged rape, and not wanting to retry the case, Judge Parks again told the jury, "It need not be a full penetration, nothing more than . . . that the private parts of the man entered to some extent into the female. . . . It does not have to be full penetration of the male organ into the vagina of the female, because, as I said there, if it is only partial, if it only penetrates to the hymen and no further, it would be sufficient under the law."

Judge Parks next addressed the legal requirement of force. The jury had been told that Dr. Stewart saw no bruises or sign of blood on Ms. Liger when he examined her immediately after the alleged incident; however, Judge Parks instructed, "It is not necessary that the force should be actual; it may be constructive force used upon the female to make her yield her consent to the intercourse."

Turning to the issue of consent, and referring to what he called a leading case, Judge Parks told the jury, "Carnal intercourse with a woman incapable from mental disease (where that disease be idiocy or mania) of giving consent is rape."

"Here," Judge Parks reminded the jury, "it is insisted by the State that . . . she did have a mania upon the subject of fortune-telling."

After summarizing once more the minimal requirement of penetration, Judge Parks returned to the issue of consent: "Now on that subject [of whether she was mentally incapacitated] I think it is entirely proper that you consider the social relation of the races, not on the question of his color, but on the question of her knowledge of the consequences of this act. If she knew that she was having intercourse with a colored man and what the possibilities or consequences that followed such intercourse might be, he didn't know, but whatever they were she was hereafter facing in her own society. Did she have the capacity to know and think upon those things? If she did not, then she would be incapacitated in giving her consent."

Did this mean the jury had to believe Elizabeth Liger understood the consequences of interracial intercourse in order to consent? If the jury believed Elizabeth Liger only had the intelligence of a twelve-year-old, then it would find she was incapable of consent and convict. But even if the jury saw Elizabeth Liger as my father saw her—as a naïve and dreamy twenty-year-old woman of average intelligence—the jury still might convict on the grounds that any Troy white woman who had intercourse with a Negro was lacking in enough walking-around sense to understand the consequences, and therefore to have given consent.

"Guilty," announced the foreman, three hours later. It was around eight o'clock that evening according to the *Messenger*. "Guilty," they all said as Judge Parks polled them one by one. "Guilty." "Guilty." Every one of them said it. Then the foreman said, "We fix his punishment at death."

The *Montgomery Advertiser* reported that "The crowd in the courtroom, which had been guarded by State Highway Patrol officers during the trial . . . received the announcement of the verdict quietly."

Chapter 27

MY FATHER TOLD ME he never doubted that his client was innocent of the crime of rape. He may have suspected that something sexual went on, but I don't recall him ever saying that. I do remember him saying something to the effect that there was no evidence of a rape, but he never to my memory used words like "intact hymen"; I only discovered those words years after his death when I procured the trial transcript.

I also remember him telling me—more than once—that the State's claim that Elizabeth Liger had the mind of a twelve-year-old was a bogus defense that the prosecutor "came up with" to challenge consent. He said he thought Elizabeth Liger was immature and silly—what we today might call an airhead—but he did not believe she was mentally incapable of consent to whatever, if anything, occurred.

I also know that my father had come to respect Charles White, and that he wanted to find a way to spare him from electrocution. There is nothing in the transcript or the record that I have been able to discover about what lawyers call an ex parte conference—a meeting between Judge Parks and my father that was not attended by

Solicitor Orme. But I recall hearing that something did occur. My surmise of what must have been said is supplemented by a curious document sent to me by a clerk of the Pike County Circuit Court in response to my request for any and all information about the case. A copy is included in the appendix.

JUDGE PARKS WAS FURIOUS with Charles White for not accepting the offer of life imprisonment with a chance for parole, and he initially did not respond when Foster asked for a few minutes to talk with his client in his cell. Judge Parks seemed to have something else on his mind, and Foster suspected he knew what it was: the judge was already beginning to feel the pressure, because some in the Troy community would not accept a judge overruling a unanimous jury's recommendation of the electric chair in order to give mercy in a black-on-white rape case. A judge could not do that if he wanted to be reelected. And not just reelected—a judge who gave mercy to a Negro for raping a white girl might best hire someone to watch his house at night. Even among the better class in Troy, who would frown on trespass to the person or property of one of their own, there would be some social ostracism of Judge Parks, and for the remainder of his years; Foster knew that was how it would be. He knew Judge Parks knew it, too. A few of his braver friends might quietly tell him—someday, over a drink—that they understood, but they likely would not speak up publicly in his defense because they would be afraid.

Judge Parks removed his black robe, loosened his four-in-hand knot, unbuttoned his collar, and drummed his fingernails on his glass-topped desk. There was evidence, the judge reminded Foster, sufficient for a jury to believe that Elizabeth Liger was a girl of limited mental development, also evidence—her testimony—that Charles White did take some kind of sexual advantage. And the law was the law when it came to an unconsented penetration. Any penetration.

Foster said nothing.

Guilt or innocence, Judge Parks said, stating the obvious, was the province of a jury, not a judge.

Foster still said nothing; just stared out a window into the starless, black Alabama night. For a few moments, there was silence.

Foster had said, the judge recalled, that Charles White wouldn't accept the plea offer because he didn't want to spend his last days in Kilby prison, didn't want to live that bad. Has he changed on that, Judge Parks wondered?

"Honestly, Judge, I don't know if he has changed on that but—"

Then, it wouldn't matter if he got the electric chair, Judge Parks mused. He'd sooner get the chair than a life sentence. The court would do him a favor by following the jury's recommendation.

Perhaps aware that he was not making any headway with his appointed defense counsel, Judge Parks opened a desk drawer and removed a single piece of paper bearing the seal of the State of Alabama: a document that would not have been admitted into evidence and was not referred to in the transcript. He gave the writing a cursory look, then slid it across his desk to Foster and watched for a reaction as the young attorney saw for the first time a list of three additional arrests of Charles White, Alias, including one for rape in Springfield, Ohio.

"Doesn't change anything for me, Judge."

What about the rape charge in Ohio, Judge Parks wanted to know?

"But it was just a charge, not even an indictment."

Judge Parks sighed and shook his head and said he didn't think Foster was made for defending capital cases. Then he told his assistant clerk he was going to give Mr. Beck a few minutes more with Charles White. The explanation was addressed to the clerk, but Judge Parks was looking at Foster, and for a flickering moment, the look was imploring, as if asking for some kind of concurrence or understanding of what necessarily was to come. In the next moment, however, the judge regained his composure. To Foster, he finally seemed at peace with whatever sentence he would announce the next day—the electric chair or life imprisonment.

MY FATHER'S principal aim in his post-trial meeting with Charles White was to convince him to ask for the mercy of the court.

"Charles, I will appeal. I will pay for the transcript. I will fight on as hard as I can. But please, please, do just one thing for me."

"What's that?"

"When Judge Parks asks if you have anything to say, ask for mercy."

"I don't know 'bout that."

"The Judge will surely go along with the jury recommendation of electrocution if you *don't* ask for mercy. He may even if you do. But he'll know it'll be easier for Troy to accept a life sentence if you've begged for mercy. And it might help us on appeal."

"Like I've been telling you all along, I don't want to live that bad."

"Charles! The judge will set your execution sometime next month."

"I'm not gonna tell that judge I did what I never did."

"I believe you."

"They'll stay my execution if you appeal," Charles said, always the expert on criminal law procedure.

"I will appeal."

"I might ask for mercy just to put that white judge to his conscience." Charles White chuckled at the thought.

"Please do that! Put him to his conscience."

IT WAS ALMOST ten thirty when Foster finally returned to his hotel, a second free night having been arranged by Judge Parks. He had to wake the unhappy little clerk, who seemed pleased to report that food was not available—not in the dining room, not through room service at such a late hour. But when Foster arrived upstairs, he found a fine supper of turnip greens, sweet potatoes, ham hock, hoecake, and blackberry cobbler in dishes laid out on his bed, courtesy, he knew, of the Negro kitchen workers and the maid. There was more than he could finish, and he wished he could have shared it with Charles White.

According to the *Montgomery Advertiser,* however, Charles White had already left Troy, taken later that same evening from the colored cell in Troy back to Kilby prison—once again "for safekeeping"—to be returned the following day to face Judge Parks at the sentencing.

THE MID-JULY HEAT on the following afternoon squatted low over the town of Troy, sparing no one, black or white. The newly tarred portions of streets in the business district were scorching and sticky to the touch; the unpaved, dusty brown alleys in the colored section were as hot as the sand on the Gulf of Mexico. Those who could do so remained indoors or sat under a tree; those who had to move moved slowly. Speech, when necessary, was short and sluggish, sentences were begun but left unfinished. Words ending in consonants were shortened—to eatin', fussin', fightin'. Longer words were heaved out, the accent on the first syllable—*in*-surance, *um*-brella—the speaker seemingly exhausted by the end of the word.

A court clerk had posted a note in the courthouse lobby that the sentencing of Charles White, Alias, would be at 2:30 p.m., a setting that allowed town and rural residents alike to have their big noon dinners and still get to court on time. But most had already had enough of Charles White. The courtroom was less than a quarter full when Charles, seeming to Foster to have aged overnight, hobbled in, the heavy black chains he was forced to wear, now that the jury had rendered its verdict, clanking with each step.

Judge Parks was probably not surprised that so few had come to watch. He must have known the community was confident of what he would do. With Charles White and his lawyer still standing, Judge Parks asked the defendant if he had "anything to say why the sentence of the law should not now be pronounced upon you?" The transcript recorded that Charles White "says nothing," but the *Messenger* reported—accurately, from what I remember being told—that he spoke up as follows.

"I wish to thank the court for its protection during the trial. I am a stranger here but believe I had a fair trial. I deny any guilt in connection with the crime, and ask for the mercy of the court."

Judge Parks glared at Foster. If Charles White wanted mercy, he should have admitted the crime and begged for forgiveness. That was how a plea for mercy was done. And what was meant by this denying any guilt "in connection with" the crime? Was he not only denying he had committed any crime, but also insinuating that the crime was Elizabeth Liger's testimony under oath? Judge Parks looked at his previously prepared notes for a moment before quickly saying, according to both the transcript and the *Messenger*, "It is the sentence of this court, founded on the jury verdict fixing your punishment at death, that you shall be put to death by electricity by causing to pass through your body a current of electricity of sufficient intensity to cause death and the application and continuance of said current through your body until you are dead. It is further ordered that the date of your execution be, and is hereby set, for Monday, the fifteenth day of August, 1938, one month from today."

Judge Parks appeared to ignore the announcement that there would be an appeal, but he must have heard what was said because, as he stood up to leave, he ruled, "Questions of law having arisen in this case for the decision of the Supreme Court of Alabama, and on motion of the defendant, it is considered, ordered, and adjudged by the court that the sentence in this case be, and hereby is, suspended, pending the defendant's appeal to the said Supreme Court of Alabama."

"All rise," called out the assistant clerk, but Judge Parks had already left his courtroom.

Chapter 28

Loss, the passed-down memory of the Lost Cause, shaped the spirit of the white South far into the twentieth century. As the years went by, the principal reason for the Civil War—to preserve slavery—gradually became an *unacceptable* reason for the War, and the loss of such a war all the more unacceptable. An *acceptable* reason for the War and the loss had to be found. Rebellion against an economic tyranny, ruthlessly imposed through punitive tariffs, became that reason. Loss of such a War by men who were gallant but vastly outnumbered—the loss by an agrarian culture to a predatory industrial juggernaut—became an acceptable kind of loss. Among the better class, the idealized model for acceptance of loss was Robert E. Lee's dignified surrender at Appomattox. As for the rough element, most of them born losers and destined to remain losers throughout their comparatively short and violent lives, loss in this life was natural, and because it was unavoidable, it had to be accepted.

Foster Beck had lost. White men who would have taken the law into their own hands on the night of the crime (had not Charles White been rushed to Kilby), who would have imposed their own false justice on the morning of the trial (but for the presence of the Highway Patrol), were now prepared to let Foster Beck be, provided he was not stiff-necked and accepted his loss. After the Scottsboro decision, someone had to represent Charles White; otherwise, the authorities would have had to turn him loose. If Foster Beck would not be admired for taking on the case when he could have gotten out of it, both the better class and the rough element would tolerate him now because he had lost. Charles White, Alias, would soon be electrocuted, and that would be the end of the matter.

Besides, there were diversions as the summer of 1938 turned to fall, beginning with football. All of white Enterprise—save only the seriously bedridden—would be at the high school's home games. Pike County Solicitor E. C. Orme, so I recall hearing, drove over from Troy to attend one of those games and came over to the Enterprise side at the half to shake hands with Foster, "to meet Miss Bertha," and to say, loudly, what a good fight Foster had put up, how he was going to make a good lawyer someday. Bertha beamed with pleasure and pride at the compliments, even though Foster said, as soon as E. C. left to shake other hands, that E. C. probably only said all that because he was thinking of running for lieutenant governor and had come to Enterprise to campaign.

Fall in south Alabama was also the time for syrup-making, a joyous annual ritual as much about socializing as about turning out buckets of fresh ribbon cane syrup. The only uncertainty was exactly when it would occur: not too early, so as to allow the cane pulp time to sweeten, but not too late: it had to be before the first killing frost. Farmers were put on the watch for a sign from the weather, town elders were consulted, and as expectations and excitement built, a weekend, usually in October, was selected. As a boy, I attended a syrup making with my father at a farm somewhere near Glenwood, and I am sure my parents went to them when they lived in Enterprise. My father insisted on going to one in the fall of 1938; it was supposed to have been a step toward normalcy in the community after the Charles White trial.

"WE HAD SYRUP MAKINGS in Weogufka, just like this one in Enterprise," Bertha said to Foster. "Sometimes, our Weogufka syrup would go to sugar and we would have rock candy at Christmas time."

They were standing together at the mill, beneath the changing fall leaves of oak and hickory trees, in the swept dirt yard of a farmhouse a mile outside of Enterprise. Six-foot-long sugar cane stalks, stripped of their leaves with machete-like knives while standing in the field, had been stacked on a mule-drawn wagon and hauled to the mill site, where local men fed them into a big stone grinder. A patient mule walked round and round while hitched to a pole connected to heavy stone rollers. The slowly revolving stones, powered by the mule, crushed and squeezed out the cane juice that was then filtered through a burlap cloth and collected in a big cooking pan that rested on a frame made from railroad irons. Beneath the iron frame was a watched hickory fire that kept the juice just short of a low boil. An apprentice helper—from time immemorial, one of the mill owner's grandsons—stood at the ready beside the cooking pan, dipping a boat paddle into the swirl, slowly moving the thickening cane juice around a series of left–right "dividers" that channeled it on its serpentine path back and forth across the pan, until it was cooked down into a crimson-black syrup and declared by the syrup master to be ready to be poured off into shiny silver-colored buckets and offered for sale.

"Bertha," Foster teased, examining a maroon-striped ribbon

cane stalk, "what you were cooking in north Alabama was not ribbon cane but sorghum, something we feed to hogs in south Alabama."

The two of them were standing off by themselves, breathing in the rich, almost too sweet aroma of the boiling cane juice—Bertha smiling, nodding, waving to friends and neighbors, sometimes being ignored in return, yet, ever the optimist, interpreting any return courtesies as a sign of forgiveness, encouraging Foster to believe that maybe he would not be resented much longer over the Charles White case; Foster, not particularly sociable by nature, judgmental of hypocrisy, frowning at the slights to Bertha, yet feigning optimism, if only not to disappoint her, whenever a man tipped his hat to her or a wife returned her smile. If Bertha would again be treated as a respected and beloved member of the community, the teacher everyone wanted for their children, then for him, the worst would have come to an end.

It was not to be. Word got around that fall that, far from accepting his loss, Foster Beck was serious about appealing, that the announcement in open court was not just for show. The thaw that Bertha imagined and that Foster hoped for became a chill. It was one thing for Foster Beck to defend a black man convicted for raping a white girl, even if he did sort of volunteer; but then to refuse to accept his loss and appeal on a lot of lawyer technicalities, that was pushing the limits of what some could tolerate.

NOTHING WAS WRITTEN DOWN and not much even had to be said out loud, but there was an "understanding" about race among whites in south Alabama, not only in 1938 but well into the 1950s and early 1960s when I was growing up in Montgomery. The understanding had come about gradually in the years following Reconstruction, the product of a compromise put into place by the better class of whites. They knew there had to be some law and order and a new image of the South if the region was to ever recover and begin to achieve prosperity, but they also recognized that the rough white element needed to let off some of the steam from time to time, else there was no telling what could happen; they might even turn on the better class. For its part, the rough element believed that periodic bull whippings, castrations, and lynchings were good ways to keep blacks in their place; but the rough element also had to make a living, and for that they had to depend on the better class. The understanding, then, came down to this: the better class would look the other way during an occasional beating or castration, even a lynching. For its part, the rough element would not go on a violent tear every damn time it felt provoked by some black person.

Foster Beck's stiff-necked insistence on appealing the verdict put the understanding to the test. In the past, the white troublemakers had been Jews or Catholics from up North who soon went back to where they came from, but this man was white, raised Methodist, and a Southerner, and he had no intention of ever leaving south Alabama. That didn't mean they could not make him leave, but the way to accomplish it had to be calibrated. This was not some redneck whose disappearance would go unnoticed, but the son of a fairly well-known, if somewhat controversial, south Alabama businessman. Violence against such a person—a lawyer to boot—could be picked up by one of the liberal papers, the *Anniston Star* or the *Atlanta Constitution,* and eventually noticed by the Yankee press, and that could tarnish the fragile new image of a progressive Alabama. The better class let it be known to the rough element that they would handle Foster Beck by shunning him, and at first, that assurance seems to have been enough.

Chapter 29

I DISTINCTLY REMEMBER pressing my father to tell me about the reactions in Enterprise to his taking on the defense of Charles White. He acknowledged that there were a few incidents. But he also told me that there were a number of fine white people in Enterprise who understood, if they did not all openly support, what he had done, and that between those relatively progressive men and women and the violent haters, there were many gradations, some defensible or at least respectable for the times, others not. Sadly, some of the sympathetic white citizens could not always forcefully and publicly condemn the violent ones—not because they endorsed violence but out of fear of retaliation against themselves or their families.

Reading between the lines of my father's refusal to condemn his beloved Enterprise, I have concluded that he initially believed that the better class had the situation under control and that the rough element would move on.

That was a misreading of the rough element. Shunning was not a practical way for them to express their discontent: they had no real social contact with a man of my father's class. On an unseasonably hot fall night, one or more of them, rumored to have been fueled by alcohol and resentment at Foster Beck's refusal to accept his loss, decided to take action.

"THE BETTER CLASS doesn't want trouble here in Enterprise," Foster said to reassure Bertha when she came to his office Saturday morning, after the incident. "Things will quiet down now."

"Those business people don't want trouble because it hurts their pocketbooks, but you won't hear those cowards say a single word in public on your behalf," Bertha said. She was not reassured. She had heard about the shattered office window, and no wonder: outside his office, for every passer-by to gape at, sat his crimson, leather-bound volumes of the *Code of Alabama* that he still owed payments on, Mr. M. L.'s fine rolltop desk, a small rug Bertha had brought from Weogufka and given to him, and two oak chairs. The nause-ating smell of the two dead animals thrown through the broken window—a possum, selected for the animal's well-known cow-ardice, and a skunk, for its offensive odor—remained heavy in the humid noon air of the office, despite repeated scourings of the walls and wood floor by the two colored women Foster had hired. The women smiled hellos to Miss Bertha and continued their labors.

"I wish you hadn't come, Bertha," Foster said, in a tone that made her sad. She sensed that he was not so much feeling defeated as embarrassed that he had been unable to defend his little domain. "Please, just leave," he said, pausing to mop sweat from his brow.

"I came to invite you to a picnic," Bertha said, her voice sprightly through the gloom.

"I have some more work to do here."

"We can finish up, Mr. Foster," called out Callie Mae, the younger of the two Negro women. "You go on with Miss Bertha."

"I mean, law work."

Bertha doubted that was true. From all she was hearing, Enterprise's better class was not giving Foster a whole lot to do.

"Then, how 'bout coming to church with me tomorrow?"

"No."

Bertha exchanged a look with Callie Mae, then she turned to go.

Foster said, "Maybe a walk Sunday afternoon, when you get back from church, if it's not raining."

MY FATHER'S CLOSENESS with money was legendary. Growing up in Montgomery, I not only heard the stories, I saw it firsthand. I remember the time—I was nine or ten—when, to my mother's embarrassment, we walked out of a restaurant in Miami Beach without ordering because my father thought all of the items on the menu were too expensive. On another family trip, this one to Washington and New York when I was eleven, I remember with great relief finally running out of the sandwiches my mother had prepared all the way back in Montgomery so that we wouldn't have to spend money going out to eat.

I am sure part of my father's reluctance to spend was attributable to those childhood Troy shopping trips when his mother argued with the train conductors and bargained with the merchants. And in 1938, with the Deep South still very much mired in the Depression, my father was not only trying to feed himself but also to prop up his profligate father's tottering timber and mercantile businesses.

Knowing how my father worried about money, and remembering my mother's optimistic nature, it's easy to fill in the blanks about their date that Sunday after church.

"I'D RATHER NOT spend the money on gas if I don't have to," Foster apologized when he came for Bertha on foot. It was sunny, but the sky was already showing clouds to the south. A drive out the paved part of the road to Dothan, in the car he shared with two other Enterprise men, would have been preferable, but, with his work drying up, he had little to spare for gas.

"Pshaw, Foster," Bertha said, "I'd much rather go for a walk. You can see things when you walk that pass by too fast in automobiles." She was wearing the same dress he had seen her in many times, dark blue with padded shoulders, splashy white print flowers and a big white collar. The dress was maybe an inch shorter than the droopy gray shrouds she wore to teach school, and it showed more of her waistline and figure. Her long black hair was pulled back, as always, in a bun, but a wisp or two had come loose and curled at her temples. He liked her hair that way and was glad she was not wearing one of her ridiculous hats to cover it up. At his suggestion, she was carrying a closed parasol in case a rain came up. In her other hand, she was holding a fruit jar filled with Miss Pauline's sweet tea and a couple of ice chips she had taken when her landlady wasn't watching.

"I couldn't think of anything else we could ..." He paused and slowed his step to speak to an approaching white couple dressed in Sunday best, on their way home from a late church service. The couple crossed over the empty road and passed them by without nodding or saying a word, the man not even tipping his hat to Bertha.

"It doesn't bother me one speck," Bertha said. Foster knew she was talking about the couple, not the heat, and that she was not being truthful. The rudeness had to have bothered her. She was social; she liked being around people, whereas he was a loner in comparison, content, if necessary, with just his family and a few good friends. And it was wrong that she was now being ostracized for what was solely his conduct; it made him mad in a way that the broken window had not.

They reached the edge of town on their walk. The small shops and the modest frame homes, some whitewashed, some not, gave way to open land, a pecan orchard on their side of the road, a pasture on the other. The wide front porch and yard of a farmhouse up ahead was empty of life save for a blue tick coon dog. The dog raised its head for just a moment, but did not otherwise stir or bark.

"I'm not going to stand for it," he said firmly.

"Do they know who broke your window?"

"I'm not talking about the window, Bertha. I mean the way they acted back there toward you. But I'm not going to let them kill Charles either. I'm going through with the appeal."

She was not as much surprised by what he said as by how he said it. Foster had always seemed to her a measured man, but now he sounded emotional, and she had not heard much of that before. "You said the appeal transcript would be expensive."

"I'll use some savings."

"I can give you close to seven dollars."

"I won't let you do that. The Court Reporter said he'll work it so I can pay in installments. I think he agrees with some of my objections, though he has to be careful letting on."

"Foster, the talk here in town is that girl was feeble-minded."

"And that's preposterous. That was what they had to come up with since there was no sign of any force. They had to show she was mentally too weak to consent."

Consent to exactly what? Bertha wanted to ask. She knew he would be embarrassed to speak of Elizabeth's condition, much less tell her who did what. People in Enterprise had heard tales that Charles bewitched Miss Elizabeth, putting some kind of a "salve" on her, but no one knew any more than that, though there were rumors: the salve was a magic potion, made from the menstrual blood of white women; the salve was a powerful aphrodisiac secreted by slaves in the galleys of the slave ships; and other such nonsense. She had not mentioned the salve before, knowing that when it came to the carnal, Foster was a lot like her father, who had used his straight razor to cut out the page with the nude male drawing from her college biology textbook. Foster was not quite that extreme, although, after three years, they were still chaste, something more important to him than to her.

Overhead, a distant slice of Alabama sky was beginning to turn dark. The cloud that had been hanging further south in Florida, over the Gulf, was coming closer. Sometimes a cloud would rain itself out over the Gulf and move on across the Florida Panhandle; other times the cloud would blow north toward Enterprise. Foster suggested they head back.

Bertha didn't want to. "I don't care if it does rain," she said, brandishing her parasol.

Foster turned to her. "Maybe he took some advantage," he said over a thunderclap as they felt the first breeze of the walk. "But he shouldn't have to die for it."

"I remember your saying before the trial that you could have done worse than Judge Parks. But sentencing Charles to death—he hasn't impressed me as such a fine man."

"I said I could have done worse back then, when I thought we had a chance. But Judge Parks buckled. All it took was for him to realize what Troy would think if he overruled the jury." Foster paused. He was afraid that he must sound as if he were making excuses for losing. "Judge Parks did some good things, bringing the Highway Patrol to Troy, the way he controlled the courtroom, kept E. C. in line. I understand the pressure he felt."

The first thin spray of rain swept over them. Bertha wiggled her parasol but did not open it. The spray felt refreshing, but they both knew it might get worse and quickened their steps back toward Miss Pauline's. There was another thunderclap, closer and louder than the first one.

"You don't buckle, Foster, you stand for what you believe. Papa would have been so proud of you for taking this case."

"And you? Are you proud of me?"

"You know I am. I hated to see you take it on because, well, I thought he was guilty at first, but after you said he was innocent—"

The first fat drops of Gulf Coast rain interrupted her. Bertha opened her parasol and took his arm, pulling him close so that each would stay at least partially dry.

As always, her praise restored his spirits and his resolve. He could ignore a little rain.

FOSTER BECK filed thirty-six Assignments of Error, the largest number anyone in Troy or Enterprise could recall in a case tried by Judge Parks, many directed to the court's admission of opinion testimony as to the mental capacity of Elizabeth Liger, and he mailed a carbon copy of all thirty-six to Charles White, who was in Kilby prison in Montgomery awaiting execution. "The truth is," Foster wrote to Charles, "I never expected we would win at trial in front of that jury. But I am very confident the Alabama Supreme Court will reverse. That is what our appellate courts are for, Charles, to look at the law dispassionately. That is the beauty of our system of law. The Supreme Court of Alabama will not allow this travesty to stand. Do not give up hope. As for me, I am more determined than ever to see justice done and am redoubling my efforts to bring it about."

Chapter 30

MY FATHER WAS hardly a stereotypical sportsman. Although he would hit feeble grounders to me in the backyard in Montgomery when I was trying out for a Little League baseball team, most of our sports interaction occurred in front of the television set on Saturday afternoons, watching Dizzy Dean announce baseball games in the summers, cheering for the Alabama Crimson Tide in the fall. My father's great passion was not baseball or football, however, but fishing in the spring and hunting in the fall. I know he hunted in and around Enterprise, and I know he attended at least one of the annual invitational dove shoots arranged by prominent local farmers with large cornfields.

"MAYBE YOU shouldn't go this year," Bertha said. "Somebody might shoot you and then say it was an accident."

"It'll be safer to go than to turn down an invitation—that is, if I get one, Bertha," he said.

The previous year's shoot had been the largest ever, with fifty carefully chosen gunners, Foster Beck among the select—he had proudly told Bertha all about it. Most of the men were from Troy, Enterprise, and Dothan, but some came from as far away as Selma and Montgomery. That year, Foster explained, as in every prior year, some corn was deliberately left unpicked, then pulled from the stalk and shucked, right there in the field, two days before the shoot. The yellow kernels lying on the ground never failed to attract doves. Because doves were a migratory bird, however, they were regulated by both the U.S. government and the state of Alabama, and "seeding" a corn field to attract doves was illegal under both jurisdictions. So, a little something had to be "left on the ground for the game wardens," as the landowner liked to put it when he passed the hat for the "admission fee."

Each year, at dawn on the day of the shoot, Negroes driving mule-drawn wagons were paid a little something to pick up white men with shotguns at the barn and deliver them to their assigned locations, the white men taking up positions a step or two back in the piney woods that surrounded the cornfield, more or less out of sight of the hungry doves. Once all the shooters were in their places, the Negro drivers returned to the barn and loaded their wagons with thick chunks of ice, ice picks, bourbon, glasses, crackling bread, and sides of barbecued pork, slow-smoked the night before. The wagon drivers circled the field throughout the rest of the day, pouring bourbon and serving pork ribs, while other paid Negroes darted out to retrieve dead or wounded birds for their assigned shooters. "Last year," Foster told Bertha with a rare chuckle, "one shooter brought a retriever. That dog would run out in the field and bring a dead bird to his master whenever he saw one fall to the ground. But the dog couldn't tell whether a falling dove was its master's or another shooter's nearby, so there were some threats to shoot the dog if it was brought back."

Foster and his twenty-gauge double-barrel had placed second in kills in 1937, the first year he was invited, and it had been understood, in view of such a fine showing, that he would be invited this year as well; and he would have been but for things heating up over the appeal. The better class—trying to keep a lid on the rough element ever since they broke Foster's office window—realized it would not be helpful to invite him in 1938.

MY FATHER would not have minded that much. I know for a fact that he much preferred the drama and the contest of quail hunting to dove shoots: walking, sometimes for hours, alone or with Tump, later with me, through miles of harvested fields, second-growth woods, and bramble, until finally Old Prince, the legendary family bird dog, a purebred pointer, would suspend his weaving and freeze, sensing the gathering covey, the birds huddling, tensing, preparing to explode in their classic shock wave of feathered thunder that never failed to startle even experienced quail hunters, the sudden, surprise burst a part of the covey's natural defense, so that if one or two birds fell to a fox or a hunter, the rest would survive to breed and replenish. Shooting lots of doves on a baited field from a fixed position had little romance to it, in my father's mind.

The lack of an invitation did leave my father without plans for the long Thanksgiving weekend. No one in Enterprise had invited him to Thanksgiving dinner, and he probably was not in a mood to face his father, who would have celebrated the holiday well into his drugs and liquor. My mother had gone to Weogufka the Wednesday after school let out to be with her mother, and Frances was in Meridian, Mississippi, with Delmas's family. Having nothing else to do, my father decided to visit Charles White in Montgomery during that Thanksgiving weekend.

CHARLES HAD BEEN MOVED from the colored incarceration section of Kilby prison to the colored death row, a string of dark, stinking, windowless cells in which two, sometimes four, Negro men awaited electrocution. He looked bad. He had lost a lot of weight, was unshaven for no telling how long, and his once coal-black steel-wool hair, unshorn since Foster paid a barber to clean him up for trial back in mid-July, had begun thinning and turning gray. Charles was lying on the wet floor in his cell when Foster found him, but he quickly struggled to his feet when he recognized his lawyer and his eyes changed from dull to flashing black.

"I'm free!" Charles said, before Foster could even say hello.

"Not yet, Charles. I just came to see how you're doing."

Charles slumped, clinging to the bars with both hands to keep from falling back onto the floor. Foster had never seen him so defeated. "*Shee-uh.* I done tol' you I don't want to live this bad."

Foster immediately noticed Charles's Southern Negro accent and poor grammar, an articulation he must have picked up from his cellmates. "Charles, you can't give up now. We're going to win this. It'll just take a little more time."

"This place ain't nothin' for a white man. What you think it like for a nigger?"

Foster had no answer for that. Instead, he said, "You've lost a lot of weight."

"Prob-ly. Couldn't help but. All I can do to eat some of the slop just to keep back the hungry pains."

One of the two other Negroes in Charles's cell got up off the floor and approached the bars where Charles White stood.

"You a law-yah, suh?" the man said. His tone was pitiful, begging.

"Git back, nigger!" Charles White shouted, pushing his cellmate away and raising a threatening arm.

"Charles, they won't give us a place to talk. I'm sorry."

For a moment, Charles seemed more focused on the possibility of beating his cellmate, even though the man had retreated. When he finally turned back to Foster, he said, "When you think we gon' hear sump'in?"

"It may be a while yet." In fact, Foster was pleased it was taking so long: people were saying it was already the longest time the Alabama Supreme Court had sat on a Judge Parks appeal. Foster tried to explain why the delay was a good sign.

"Yo' brief was powerful," Charles said. "I'm hidin' it here under my mattress till you need it back."

"No, Charles, you can keep that carbon copy. The Supreme Court has the original, and I have another carbon at my office." Foster wondered what Charles would say if he knew the reason the brief read so well: because of Bertha's edits. She had come to his office after school to read and revise his drafts, and it was soon apparent that she had superior knowledge of the rules of good grammar; perhaps more important, Foster thought she added an almost musical flow to his chop-chop analytical arguments.

"That solicitor wrote anything back?"

"Nothing to speak of, Charles. As I said, I'm very confident we have the better of it." Foster was in fact very confident. Even the lawyers in Troy were saying that this time, Judge Parks might get reversed; Foster wanted to say more about all that to Charles, but he was torn. He didn't want to get Charles's hopes up too high, but at the same time his client needed encouragement. Charles implored him with his eyes to say more, and Foster gave in. "It's not just me. Other lawyers are saying the Supreme Court's going to reverse. But it won't do a speck of good if you don't hold on and take care of your health."

Charles's countenance lifted a little with the assurance. Foster knew his client would have vigorously cross-examined him before the trial, but now he was reduced to grasping at the thin offerings. Foster was beginning to understand why Charles always said he didn't want to live that bad; it was not his first time behind bars, and Alabama's Negro ward was doubtless worse than the places where he had served time up North. For the first time, Foster was beginning to worry that Charles might give up and take his own life. Suicide was not unheard of at Kilby prison, especially among the Negroes kept there.

"They turn me loose, I won't be stayin' in Alabama for the next sunrise," Charles said. He seemed already to be dreaming of living in Chicago or Detroit, anywhere but Alabama. Foster decided not to warn him that a reversal wouldn't necessarily mean he was free to go and probably would mean a retrial, as Judge Parks had threatened; it was better not to say all that to Charles just yet. Maybe he could get him released on bail after the Alabama Supreme Court reversed. Provided he didn't kill himself first.

Chapter 31

THE FIRST EXTENDED cold snap marked the time for hog killings in rural Alabama. The killing, bleeding, gutting, scraping to remove the hair, and butchering had to be done in a single, long, cold day so the meat would not spoil before it could be salted, smoked, and cured.

My father wrote about the butchering of hogs in our family history. "When it was time to kill hogs [my mother] would send for Aunt Missouri and Uncle Berry, faithful black friends, and together they would stuff and season the sausage, prepare the hams and shoulders for curing, clean the chitterlings, cut up the backbone and render the fat into lard. We would pester her until she sliced off a piece of tenderloin and quickly fried it for us over the coals. It was a custom then for those killing hogs to send their neighbors some fresh meat. So, Mama would wrap pieces of backbone, tenderloin and cracklins in a piece of newspaper and I would carry it to the neighbors. It was a day light to dark job for all, but my, how good that fresh meat was."

I never got to witness an entire hog killing from dawn to dusk, even though we made frequent weekend trips throughout the 1940s and 1950s to Glenwood, but I saw enough. And as was always the case growing up in the South, I heard the stories passed around, especially about the killings that were not just family but community events. There likely would have been several such community hog killings on the farms around Enterprise in 1938. I know that my parents attended one of them, and I know this because of the part I was told was played by my mother.

THE MAYHEM, blood, and gore of hog killings discouraged squeamish girls, even some of the boys and men, from wanting to see it more than once. Bertha Stewart was not squeamish but she had refrained, after her first one, from attending further killings because she saw "nothing uplifting" in the ritual, so Foster was surprised when Bertha said, "I'm going to a hog killing this year."

"I don't think that's a good idea," he said. "And I know why you are saying you want to go."

"I'm not going to let them sideline us. We need to go for a while just to show our faces."

And so, at the crack of first light, Bertha, along with Foster and six other men, gathered at the chosen hog farm to do what needed to be done. A .22 rifle, used rather than a more powerful gun or an axe in order to minimize damage to the prized brains, was carefully aimed and fired by each of the men into a marked spot between each animal's eyes. After some teasing about her owl kill off the back porch years before in Weogufka, Bertha took a turn and succeeded in killing a hog.

The next step was to bleed and gut the dead animals. The hind legs of each three-hundred-pound or greater hog carcass were carefully tied to one end of a strong rope, and the other end was thrown over a sturdy hickory branch, then hitched to a team of mules which hoisted the dead hog up off the ground. As each hog corpse swung in the cold air, the hog owner stuck a big, sharp butcher knife into a carefully chosen artery and then got out of the way fast as the blood spouted and sprayed. Once the bleeding was done, the hog farmer used the same trusty knife to slice open the belly, being careful not to nick the intestines, which were removed and placed in pots of cold water until they could be cleaned and preserved for those who favored chitterlings.

By the time the gutted and bled hog bodies were hauled by mule-drawn wagons to the butchering site, the large black cast iron scalding vats had been heated over a wood fire and were beginning to steam, but not boil. The water had to be the right temperature—hot but not too hot—or the hair wouldn't "slip." At some point, the hog farmer's wife took charge and supervised the transfer of the hairless pink and gray carcasses as they were lifted and laid on the scrubbed cutting table used every year. There, the hog was blocked with an axe into parts small enough, at thirty or so pounds, to be carved into hams, pork chops, ribs, and bacon by the strong and experienced women who had come to help.

Bertha was unsure she could handle the unwieldy chunks of slippery hog meat while at the same time using a sharp knife, and she was relieved when, with a contemptuous glare, one of the older farm women turned down her offer to help. Partly it was because the woman did not want the high school Shakespeare teacher to ruin the cuts of pork, but there was also a chill, and not just owing to the cold snap. Word had gone around that Foster had used his Thanksgiving holiday to visit the nigger rapist at Kilby, and that was not appreciated by the better class and was all but intolerable to the rough element, both classes being well represented at hog killings. Believing she had made her point, Bertha was glad to have to leave to teach *Macbeth*, and to have papers on *Lear* to grade as her excuse for not returning in the afternoon to watch the shoulder trimmings being ground into sausage, seasoned, and stuffed into casings made from the hogs' intestines, to see the fat cooked down into lard, to gather a share of the crispy residues for winter use in crackling bread.

MID TO LATE DECEMBER was about the time word got around that Foster Beck had not just visited his guilty nigger rapist in Kilby but had paid for the appeal transcript with his own money. Even among some of the better class, this latest revelation was resented. The rough element, picking up the scent, took their betters' discontent as a nod and a wink that it would be all right for them to do something.

On a cold day the week before Christmas, three strong-backed brothers decided to teach Foster Beck a lesson. They found him fishing on a creek bank late in the afternoon, alone because no one wanted to fish with him, and when he ignored their taunts, they pushed him down on the muddy bank and called him "nigger lover." When he still wouldn't fight back, they pushed him into the cold water and then stood on the bank and peed all along the edge. When he finally became angry enough to try to fight his way out of the creek, they pushed him back down into the water, over and over, and held him under water for a while, until finally they became a little embarrassed at his stubborn efforts to resist. Still, they might not have let him come out of the water until dark, but the late December chill got so bad the brothers had to leave.

When the story of what happened on the creek bank got around, the self-respecting folks let it be known, without having to make an issue of it, that enough was enough. They knew from experience that if they let the creek incident pass, it would whet the appetite of the rough element for more; violence was like a contagion with them, and it could get out of control. Besides, Foster Beck had not been intimidated by the window-breaking or the creek bullying; more of that sort of thing probably would not turn him around. On the other hand, everybody knew Foster worried about money. To placate the rough element, some of the better class spread around that Foster Beck's retainer from one of his best-paying clients was being eliminated, and that there would be less paying legal work in the future. They also began musing over ways to get at Bertha.

"Course I won't press charges," Foster said to Frances, who heard about the creek incident with the three brothers. "That would just keep it going. If I were to press charges, they would circle the wagons."

"That's ridiculous, Foster. They obviously are unified already."

"That's just the hardheads. The fact is, the whites in this town are not of one mind on race. It's just like Daddy always said, the South's not solid, just different. The business people, the educated ones, understand somebody had to defend Charles White after Scottsboro, and they're the ones who feel like now it's time to leave me alone and move on."

"If you won't press charges, I will," Frances said. She was hopping mad. "They might kill you next time."

"No, Frances, that won't happen. They just needed to let off a little steam. Things'll cool off now." He was convinced the worst had finally blown over.

Chapter 32

I T WAS DURING that December of 1938 that the relationship between my parents began to change. They had been seeing each other for at least three years by then, but my father, concerned about his declining law practice, had still not proposed marriage, and my mother, who worried far less than he did about money, was becoming impatient.

I learned about those tensions years later from my beloved Aunt Frances, who feared my mother was not going to wait much longer in a town that had never really been her home and was over a hundred miles from Weogufka and her mother, Mrs. Stewart.

SOMETIME BEFORE school let out for Christmas in 1938, Frances arranged for the three of them to meet for supper. Miss Pauline would be at prayer meeting at the Baptist church until at least nine o'clock and didn't mind if Bertha used the kitchen and dining room as long as she cleaned up. Frances came early and cooked the chicken dumplings for which she was famous; Bertha made peach cobbler, her only good dish.

"I can't afford a wife right now, Frances," Foster whispered while Bertha was getting the plates and silverware, for a brief moment out of earshot. "My clients who can pay cash money have cut back." He paused and shook his head. "The business people say I'm being 'stiff-necked.'"

"The ones who say that don't know their Bible," Bertha said, overhearing the accusation as she returned with the dishes and began to set the table. Electricity, though still unavailable in much of rural Coffee County, had come to the town of Enterprise, though it was new and used sparingly by Miss Pauline, who grew up at a time when oil lamps were required in the evenings. Knowing Miss Pauline would be at church for another two hours, Bertha had glee-fully turned on the ceiling light that hung over the dining table. "God told Moses His people acted stiff-necked when they disobeyed His laws by making the Golden Calf. You don't disobey any of the laws, Foster."

"He may not disobey but he can be stubborn," Frances said in good humor. It had begun to storm, and the wind blew the rain in gusts against the bay window in the dining room. "But I can't see why your being stubborn would make them want to bring you down. It's what you did for a colored man they don't like, not your attitude."

"Frances, listen to me. Daddy warned me about all this last sum-mer. He said the good white people want to change but are afraid to change too fast. Daddy said that jury would think I was trying to change things too fast and resent it coming from one of their own. And I've come to think Daddy was right, even though he was drink-ing right there on the office porch, in broad daylight, even though some of it made no sense. You know how he can be."

Frances did not confirm or deny. "What else did he say?"

"He has this idea that today's good Southern white people are deep-down ashamed of how their granddaddies fought to defend slavery."

Frances turned to Bertha and laughed. "He's talking about *south* Alabama granddaddies, not the ones where you're from up in north Alabama." She was thinking of the scalawag Stewart ancestors, who had had no slaves and refused to fight for the Confederacy.

"Oh, but we had that on the Rayfield side," Bertha said. "Great-granddaddy Rayfield didn't have any slaves, but he still managed to lose a leg for General Lee."

Outside, the rain whipped in bursts against the window. A sudden flash of light was followed quickly by explosive thunder, signaling that the storm was close, and for a moment the room went dark; then the electric light came back on. Foster lit the oil lamp, just in case. "Daddy said I understand ideas but not people."

"Maybe he was right, Foster. I mean, about the need to understand people. Maybe they *are* ashamed and think you are judging them and they don't like it one bit."

"I'm not judging anybody, Bertha. I'm just doing what the Constitution and a decent society requires, defending a Negro entitled to a lawyer—"

"But maybe what they don't like," she interrupted, "is not that you defended him. They could put up with that. It's because you haven't forgiven them. They see that as . . . as un-Christian of you."

The charge took Foster by surprise. After a pause, he said, "I don't know what on earth you are talking about, Bertha. Forgiving them? I'm a lawyer, not a preacher, and I—"

"If you went to church some you would know about forgiveness," she again interrupted. "Maybe all they really want is to be seen as ordinary Americans, guilty of other sins, yes, just like all ordinary Americans are, but forgiven for the unique historic sins of their grandfathers. Maybe that's why they embrace Christianity so fervently, with its promise of forgiveness."

"I thought you churchgoers believed you had to repent to earn forgiveness. You see any of those whites repenting?"

"You both might have made a preacher, but neither one of you would last long around here," Frances said the moment they stopped interrupting each other and she could get a word in. She was hoping to break the rising tension, but Bertha did not laugh and Foster did not even smile.

"You're not from around here, Bertha," he said. "There are no Negroes in Weogufka. South Alabama's different. The whites around here are outnumbered and afraid of change that comes too fast."

"Maybe that's just an excuse."

"Like I said, you're not . . ." Foster stopped and shook his head. "But you can at least understand this: if you were a Negro, you might want some revenge, not just change. I know I might. The good whites here in Enterprise know that too, and feel trapped, and the thing is, I understand all that. And I hate it that we are trapped like this—"

"But Foster, the final answer can't be that we are forever trapped, that we do nothing?"

"That's not what I meant, and you know it."

"Of course you are doing something, and it is important and brave. I was going to say all that next, but you interrupted—"

"And you interrupted me. You say the answer can't be that we forever do nothing, but then when I do something, you say I'm stiffnecked for not forgiving them—"

"I didn't say you are that way. I said people here think that you are." Bertha got up and collected the dirty dishes.

After another stretch of silence, Foster began to feel badly about the way he had spoken and to wish he could take some of it back. He would "forgive" them all—whatever she meant by that—if doing so would bring the town's respect back to her and a return of the modest prosperity he had enjoyed before taking the case, which, like a disease, had paralyzed his little law practice. But instead of saying any of that, he thanked Bertha and Frances for the meal and got up to leave.

"I'm not sure I can keep my practice open much after New Year's," he blurted out to Frances at the door. It was humiliating; he had vowed to avoid the financial difficulties of his father, and here he was, about to lose everything.

"You know, two can live as cheaply as one," Frances said, still hoping to salvage the evening.

Foster knew exactly what Frances meant by that but remained silent. He had too much pride to ever let Bertha support him, even if they could get by just on her salary and what little he was still bringing in. Not knowing when, if ever, the town's resentment would subside, he was hesitant to offer her false hope for the future, though he suspected that, even without Frances's hectoring, Bertha was coming to the end of her patience with him. He couldn't blame her.

For her part, Bertha could have strangled Frances for saying two could live as cheaply as one. And she was a little sorry to have argued with Foster about forgiveness and church, but the fact was, she *had* been loyal and supportive throughout the ordeal with Charles White. And besides, things were changing for her, too. Her father's death had left her mother alone and solely responsible for the Weogufka farm. While Mrs. Stewart had cancelled her late husband's subscriptions to science journals and sold off the exotic birds and animals he had bred, without his steady salary as a mail carrier, she barely had enough money for the few necessities she couldn't raise in the pasture or grow in the garden; and always there were the land taxes.

Bertha knew her mother's situation and was sure she could find a teaching position in Rockford or Sylacauga—even Montgomery would be a lot closer to home than Enterprise—and she was beginning to wonder if Foster would ever commit to her, if not for one reason, then for another. She was beginning to resent him for that. At first it had been just a little resentment, but it was growing, and besides, she had her pride and didn't want to keep hint-hinting around.

Foster was the right one for her, she knew that, and he also was likely the only one who would ever appreciate a woman her age who was sometimes described, not necessarily as a compliment, as "regal," and always pigeonholed as a poor cook and bookish and a little too much on the independent side—for example, wanting to keep her own checkbook. Things like that annoyed other men, so they would never ask her out more than once or twice, much less to marry. Bertha was afraid to bring things to a head with Foster and possibly end their courtship, and yet she was afraid to do nothing and become a year older. In the meantime, she was feeling a need to look after herself.

"I'm going to have to spend more weekends at home," she said after Foster said he might not be able to keep his office open much after the New Year. "Mama's having a hard time managing by herself." It was the best she could do for an excuse to end the conversation.

Outside, the rain slacked up; the lightning and thunder had finally moved east, blowing toward the Chattahoochee River and Georgia. By the time Miss Pauline returned from prayer meeting to find the electricity turned off and Bertha and Frances reading by the oil lamps, the sky was clear and cold.

Chapter 33

"CHRISMUS GIF, young Cap'n. You shore is the spittin' image of the ole Cap'n."

As a child, I heard that exact greeting from Pete Tate on many a Christmas morning in Glenwood, the custom being that the first one to say "Christmas gift" was supposed to receive one. My father told me that he, too, heard it when he was a boy, a reminder that Glenwood was slow to change. Though some things did change—the dime he always gave Pete Tate had become a quarter from me.

My father enjoyed telling me about Christmases when he was a boy in Glenwood, the home filled with family and other celebrants from throughout the county, the sounds of laughter and carols, the mouthwatering smells. On Christmas mornings, his father, "the ole Cap'n," would give Pete a good slug of Four Roses, and his mother, Miss Lessie, would fix Pete a big plate of sausage, eggs, biscuits, and ribbon cane syrup, and round up some spare clothes for him and his family. Pete would bestow his own gift by cutting a load of firewood and laying a good fire.

By the time my father tried the Charles White case, Christmases in Glenwood had become more somber occasions. For one thing, Mr. M. L.'s contacts with the local white community had begun to wither, and no wonder. As recorded in our family history, my grandfather, tolerant of different opinions about some issues, would get into nearly violent arguments over others, saying unforgivable things, then act surprised that his former adversary was hurt with him since he himself did not hold grudges and therefore did not expect others would.

The bourbon and cocaine and whatever else my grandfather used to combat his melancholia—both the kind of mental depression he had always suffered and the kind that was new, brought on by advancing age—also took a toll. My father told me that his bouts of optimism one day, pessimism the next, had become steadily more unpredictable and pronounced. Sometimes, he would seem suspended in a lugubrious haze, other times he was vigorous, high as a kite, captured by his own impossible dreams—one of the most memorable being his long fascination with tracts of timber land in Brazil. My grandfather had read somewhere about millions of acres of virgin rain forest in Brazil, and the thought of all those tall trees waiting to be harvested had temporarily restored the old sawmill man's appetite for money and adventure. For years, I was told, books and envelopes containing colorful pamphlets arrived at the house in Glenwood, extolling the beauty and mystery of Brazil and the opportunities there for an experienced lumberman.

FOSTER WAS SAD, when he arrived in Glenwood for Christmas in 1938, to see the latest envelopes about Brazil piling up in the hallway unopened, for that meant his father's final dream was nearing an end. Stepping over stacks of books and magazines in the dimly lit library, he reached to awkwardly hug his father, who was seated in his chair. Mr. M. L. looked up, startled, but did not stand or return the embrace. Instead, he began groping among the unpaid bills on the oak table beside his chair. His shaking hand knocked over the little bell he'd been looking for, and the clatter, as it hit the floor and rolled under the sofa, brought Pete to his side. Mr. M. L. held up a gnarled forefinger, about three inches apart from the crooked thumb he had injured a decade ago at the sawmill—his signal to Pete to pour him three inches of Four Roses. "Shame," Mr. M. L. muttered as he turned to his son. "Shame eats at us like acid."

Pete came with the three inches in a crystal glass, part of a set of fine crystal used only on holidays. The set had been part of the marriage dowry of Lessie Mae Beck, née Lessie Mae Moxley, the beautiful and brilliant daughter of Dr. D. N. Moxley, the Confederate Army surgeon, and Sarah Narcissus King. After the war, Dr. Moxley settled near Glenwood and, according to the family history, practiced medicine on horseback within a range of twenty miles, pulling teeth for fifty cents, delivering babies for four dollars, making house calls for one to two dollars plus a small charge per mile, and accumulating fifteen hundred acres of land, including eight hundred acres in the Conecuh River swamp, where he kept a drove of wild hogs. The Moxleys belonged to a higher social class than the Becks, and eyebrows had been raised when Miss Lessie Moxley married Madison Lewis Beck.

"Shame!" Mr. M. L. repeated, holding the Moxley crystal at arm's length and frowning at it, as if looking for an imperfection in the glass.

Foster, unprepared for how much his father had declined, waited in silence. Outside, the winter sun had almost gone down.

"Light the wick," Mr. M. L. ordered when he could not find the bell to summon Pete. Although there was electricity in Glenwood, Mr. M. L. sentimentally preferred the oil lamps of his childhood. Foster lit the wick and retrieved the bell.

Mr. M. L., still holding the crystal aloft, admired the whiskey glowing orange-brown in the lamplight. For a moment, he seemed to be trying to remember why he'd brought all this up about shame. Foster wondered, too.

"A shame they try to expiate these days," his father continued, "by resort to quackery. They ignore men like my friend Carver. They refer to the quackery, and they say, 'We in the South are *working on it*, but the Negro's not yet *ready* for equal treatment. You've heard 'em say that about the Negro not being ready."

"Daddy, I'm not sure what all of this—"

"They *say* the Nigra's not ready because they're *ashamed* of not changing how things are."

Foster took a seat across the library from his father and waited.

"Of *course* some of the Negroes aren't ready. I've been inside the Nigra schools here in Crenshaw County. They don't have as many books as are here in my library."

"That's true."

"Some of those Negro children, though, would do just as well as the good white students and better than your poorer ones. But nobody says the poor white students aren't 'ready' and ought to be sent to a worse school with no books."

"Daddy, I agree all that's so—"

"Everything I'm saying is so. And the decent ones know it's so. That's how come they're ashamed. But they don't want to hear about any change from one of their own. No sir. Doesn't matter if he's a Hard Shell, a Methodist, a Catholic or a Jew, if he's white and Southern, they can't abide hearing about it. That's how they saw you, son, as one of their own, and that's why you lost that case."

My father said he didn't argue or try to defend himself that Christmas. Upon thinking about it, I'm not surprised. The thought that a Yankee lawyer—someone who was not "one of their own"— might have done better would have made him feel all the worse for Charles White.

There also was, so I've heard, some tension that Christmas about my mother. As the father of two daughters, both of whom he had sent to college, Mr. M. L. was comfortable around educated women such as my mother. Maybe that Christmas, he put some pressure on my father to propose. Years later, my mother would laugh at "the very idea," and tell me "Mr. M. L. just wanted a male heir to carry forward the Beck name."

I do know that during that Christmas holiday, my grandfather gave my father a gold coin that he had inherited from his own father, Joseph Beck, who joined an Alabama regiment when he was fourteen years old and went off to fight for the Confederacy. I'm not sure, though, of the motive for the gift. The family joked that after President Roosevelt's decision to devalue gold, Mr. M. L. didn't think the coin would be worth a damn. I prefer to think the gold coin was meant as an early wedding gift.

For sure, Pete Tate and Tump Garner would have said nothing about a wedding that Christmas Day: the subject of white people's personal lives, like race relations, was way off limits. Tump, though, indirectly said a little something about the Charles White case.

"We appreciative for what you doin', Mr. Foster," Tump told my father. It was the day after New Year's, the second day of 1939, and the two of them and Old Prince were quail hunting. The men were standing, Daddy told me years later, on furrows at the edge of a ploughed-under cotton field that would lie fallow until spring, beneath a winter-blue, cloudless sky, a light breeze from the west, the temperature in the mid-thirties. Old Prince, frisky at the promise of another hunt, was weaving back and forth into the second-growth piney woods, nose to the ground in search of a covey. My father knew what Tump meant, and always cherished his memory of that moment: the fine weather, the dog, the hunt, the fact that nothing more needed to be said.

Chapter 34

FOSTER HAD ASKED BERTHA to spend a few days of the Christmas and New Year's holiday with him in Glenwood, but she claimed that she was needed at home, even though her brother Lincoln would be there for a while before returning to Fitzgerald, Georgia. And she had not suggested that Foster visit her in Weogufka. Foster was beginning to feel a chill and to suspect that he was going to have to commit to her sometime soon or risk losing her.

That was the risk Frances meant to convey when she told him that Bertha was now seriously thinking about going to the New York World's Fair as soon as school was out, maybe even looking for a job up there. Foster knew Bertha didn't tell Frances much and that Frances would exaggerate to serve a purpose, such as prodding him to propose marriage. But Bertha going to the 1939 New York World's Fair did not sound like a threat—more like exactly the sort of thing Bertha would light on doing. In truth, he was a little hurt that she had not already told him herself. But that changed shortly after New Year's, when he received a letter Bertha had written and mailed while she was still in Weogufka for the holidays.

Sadly, I have never found the letter, but I heard about it. Given the stories she told about the trip and my knowledge of my mother, I'm sure that the letter brimmed with excitement. Mother had been reading all she could find about New York City, which she had wanted to visit since she was a girl, and the theme of the Fair, "Dawn of a New Day," greatly appealed to her optimistic nature. I do know she cleared the trip with her mother, Mrs. Stewart, who urged her to go, insisting she would "do just fine"; and I do not doubt that she reminded Mother for the umpteenth time that Grandma Rayfield farmed that rocky piece of land with a one-legged Confederate husband and a boy who couldn't reach the plow handles.

SO THERE IT WAS: a letter saying she was going to New York as soon as summer vacation began. And she was telling him she was going, not asking about doing it, and in a letter that pretty much said there was no point trying to change her mind. Also, there was a postscript. If she got a job, she might be gone all summer.

"Maybe gone forever," Frances warned when he showed her the letter.

"I doubt it, Frances." He expected just such a reaction from his sister. "For one thing, she would never want to be that far from Mrs. Stewart."

"She says in the letter her mother told her to go on to New York. Mrs. Stewart said she could manage just fine. And for another thing, she may not have a job for the next school year. Bertha's in big trouble with the superintendent."

"I already know about that, Frances. It's nothing. All she has to do is give his grandson an A. That's not big trouble."

"She won't give him an A, and it has turned into something. But

it's not just because of the grade. You know why they're really pushing this, don't you?"

He knew: it was a way for some in the better class to pressure him
either to stop acting stiff-necked or get out of town.

"But she has to teach, Foster. You know how she is about wanting to teach."

Foster thought of saying that sometimes people could not do
exactly what they wanted to do, but instead had to do what it took
to make a living. But he saw his sister's reply coming from a mile
away: how he had done what he wanted to do, taking on the Charles
White case.

"Of course I know how Bertha is about wanting to teach, Frances. I know her better than you do. But I also know what you are up
to. And I can't support myself and Daddy these days, much less her
too, so she needs to keep her job. She doesn't need to be taking on the
Coffee County school superintendent tonight." He was referring to
a school board meeting called for that evening, just before classes
resumed after the Christmas holidays, to resolve the coming year's
budget problems—maybe by letting a couple of teachers go.

As a boy, I remember hearing more than once about the county
superintendent's demand that his grandson receive a better grade.
Even years later, when we lived in Montgomery, my mother's voice
would shake when she spoke of the threat; it was one of the two
times—the other was when she visited me in Atlanta several months
after my father's death—that I saw tears in her eyes. She resented the
superintendent's bullying, she really cared about teaching, and, of
course, she wanted to, had to, keep her job.

I have no written record of the meeting in Enterprise. I have to believe, however, that some parents would have stood up for her that night. I know she was seen as a truly superb teacher. While research-ing this book—more than half a century after my mother last taught in the Coffee County schools—an elderly Enterprise man with whom I spoke brought up, without prompting, that she was a much respected and beloved teacher. And without question she had that reputation as a teacher at Morningview School throughout my childhood in Montgomery. At Christmas, my mother would receive cards and letters from men and women throughout the South, including one letter from a partner at a big law firm in Washington, D.C., extolling her virtues, claiming she was the best teacher they'd ever had. Years after my mother passed away, I was having lunch at Atlanta's Commerce Club when a prominent businessman asked if I was really Bertha Stewart's son, then praised her teaching in the same superlatives.

But when it comes to my mother's reputation as a teacher, what I remember most of all is her funeral in Montgomery. After my younger daughter played a composition on the piano in the Meth-odist church, I walked toward the pulpit. The new preacher, who had transferred to our church during my mother's final two years in an Atlanta nursing home, had not known Mother, and so she asked me to say a few words. And I remember thinking, *the minister is a woman*—the first female preacher in that church. My mother would have been so proud!

As I was just about to begin speaking, I saw four elderly guests, three women and one man, come hobbling down the aisle on walk-ers, looking for an empty pew. I stepped down from the pulpit to meet them, and when I asked how they knew my mother, one of the women, whose name was Mabel, said she had been a student in

Eclectic, where Mother had taught before moving to Enterprise. Of course I asked her to tell the congregation about my mother, and this is what she said, addressing the congregation from the pulpit.

"Miz Beck—I called her Miz Stewart in those days—knew I loved books, loved to just handle books, but we didn't have books on our farm in Eclectic. So she let me begin staying after class to reshelve books in the school library."

In the church in Montgomery that day of my mother's funeral, you could have heard a pin drop. I know I was transfixed.

"One afternoon," Mabel said. Her voice caught, and she trembled but continued, "I'd finished reshelving the books and was leaving to go home. Miz Stewart called out, 'Mabel, what's that book you're takin' with you?' I showed the book. Miz Stewart fussed at me. 'Mabel, that's not a *big* book. I want you to read *big books*, Mabel.'"

Mabel again stopped and caught a deep breath. "Miz Stewart took that book from me and laid it aside and took me by the hand to a shelf and said, '*This* is the sort of book you should read from now on, Mabel. This is a *big* book.'"

For a moment, Mabel's nervousness seemed to have returned, but then she plunged ahead. "The book Miz Stewart gave me was *The Forsyte Saga*. It was a big book all right. It took me nearly a month to get through all of it because it was so long, and I had to help at home. But by the time I did get through it, I had come to understand what Miz Stewart was meaning by it being a *big* book. Not just a long book. From that time on, I did as she said and only read big books." Mabel looked at the congregation, then turned to the first woman to be a minister in the church, and said, "Miz Stewart changed my life."

———

I'M NOT CERTAIN if my father went to the school board meeting that night. If he did not attend, it would have been to spare my mother the taint of being seen in public with him; she would have had enough on her hands without that. If he did go, he'd have sat in the back, out of sight, where he could have glimpsed the back of her neck as she lowered her head in embarrassment when—as surely must have occurred—one after another, the parents of Coffee County rose to extol my mother's teaching skill.

Whatever was said that night must have sufficed, because my mother did not lose her job in Enterprise—and she never changed that grade.

Chapter 35

THE CONTINUED DELAY by the Alabama Supreme Court in ruling on my father's appeal on behalf of Charles White gave him hope in the spring of 1939. There was speculation, as the weeks turned into months, that the delay could only mean one thing: the Supreme Court—not the Yankee-appointed Supreme Court in Washington, but the elected Alabama Supreme Court—was taking the appeal seriously.

Was my father's cautious optimism justified? After reading the transcript more than once and thinking about what he said and didn't say, I have come to regard *State of Alabama v. Charles White, Alias* as a riddle—like one of those Russian dolls that, as each outer shell is removed, reveals a another figure nesting inside. There could only have been a rape if intercourse was forced, and Elizabeth Liger showed no signs of bruises or blood; but the law also recognized use of "constructive" force. There could only have been a rape if there was penetration, and she was intact; but any unconsented penetration could amount to rape. Was Elizabeth Liger's mentality really that of a twelve-year-old, or, as my father repeatedly insisted, was that an excuse the State came up with so that whatever happened must have been done without her lawful consent? And what did happen? A clue may reside in the testimony about the salve.

Charles White was a healer, so he likely would have carried salves and potions in his medicine bag. Did Southern white women use salves, not just medicinally but for other purposes, in private? Elizabeth Liger could have asked Charles White, after he told her fortune, to give her a little of the salve in his medicine bag, show her how to use it. I doubt he would have applied it to her private parts—he swore he didn't. But even applying it herself, especially in his presence, could later have given her guilty second thoughts, leading her to claim she had been raped. And a Troy jury in 1938 might not have stood for a black man touching a white woman that way or teaching her how to touch herself. Charles White had to be punished for doing something unspeakable, something that could not be tolerated.

Would my father have been able to convince a unanimous jury to acquit if the two black men who were called had been impanelled? I doubt it. Such men in those days would have known they could be bull-whipped or worse if they didn't go along.

Would the verdict have been different if women had been allowed to serve—would women have better understood the temptations of a salve? I will never know, although I remember an intriguing comment my father once volunteered, when we were talking about the case, almost as an apology for losing the trial. He told me, in a tone of voice I remember as embarrassed, that Alabama women were not allowed to serve on felony case juries in 1938. Thinking back on it, I wonder if he thought that some women on the jury might have been more understanding about the salve?

In my forty-four years as a lawyer, I have never known anyone who more thoroughly enjoyed the practice of law than my father. I think it was for him a match of the intellectual, the practical, and the compassionate. But I do not think that my father's law practice was thriving in 1939, despite the fact that he had kept the Alabama Supreme Court at bay for so long. I gather he did do a little criminal law work—and, ironically, for some of the rough white element, who still didn't like him but called on him anyway because he was good. Also, he gave them time to pay. And he still had his loyal black clients. But neither the poor whites nor the black clients had much cash money to spare; they only had what little was left in ribbon cane syrup from the syrup making, or in salt pork from the hog killing, or what they had put up from their gardens; and I remember my father saying he already had plenty of all that from previous cases he had taken. Yet he would not turn down his clients' meager offerings, because he wouldn't offend their pride—that was another thing he told me more than once when I was a boy: *never offend another man's pride.*

As for the folks who could pay, some of them—for, as Mr. M. L. always said, the white South was not of one mind about race—asked him to draw up a contract, close a real estate sale, or write a will. But this work was spotty and low-paying.

Besides worrying about making a living, my father also worried, in the last days of April 1939, that Charles White was going to take his own life if the Alabama Supreme Court didn't hurry up. But if my father made another trip to Kilby prison to encourage Charles to hang on, I have no record of it. I imagine him instead staying put in

Enterprise, living as frugally as possible, going to his office every day in hopes someone would crack the screen door and ask him a question he could charge a decent amount to answer; and when no clients came, reading his favorite book, *Plutarch's Lives*, which had been given to him by my mother, and other good books borrowed from the school library.

I do know that when he found a thought he especially admired in those days, he recorded it in his "Common Place Book"—a little notebook, now in my possession, that he had been keeping since college. Among the dozens of quotations by such authors as Plato, Aristotle, and John Stuart Mill is the following, the very first entry, reproduced without attribution. "Unless superior gifts are linked with a strong sense of social obligation, their possession is a menace rather than a blessing to society."

In lighter moods, my father might have returned to the heroic wild animal stories by Ernest Thompson Seton that he had read as a child, and when he tired of them, to the *Saturday Evening Post*, which he read cover to cover—he told me it cost only a nickel back then. And always, since much of the news focused on Europe, he would have been glad to get the *Atlanta Constitution*, even if it arrived two days late.

When his one good eye got too tired to read any more, he would have gone fishing alone, preferring his own society to the poor company willing to fish with him. The walk to the creek would have refreshed him, even if the bream, his favorites, were not biting. The trees that had been dark gray all winter must have been putting out tiny new light green leaves, as they did every April; and although it would have been a few more days before his favorite magnolias had reached their peak, he could have admired, in the meantime, the sprays of dancing white dogwood flowers suspended in the cool April air, and the sudden explosions of red and pink Pride of Mobile azaleas ornamenting the front yards of white and black Enterprise alike.

On the last day of April 1939, he received the envelope that changed forever his views about the law.

Chapter 36

BACK BEFORE THE INTERNET, whenever I received an opinion in the mail from a higher court, I would tear open the envelope and turn first to the end to see how it came out. If my father did the same, he would have read these words from *State of Alabama v. Charles White, Alias*: "Affirmed, all justices concur."

But, of course, affirmed; *unanimously* affirmed. Why had he allowed himself to dream of any other result—because he believed the majesty of the law extended to a colored man? For a minute or two, he had no appetite for reading even one more word of the opinion, only numbness and dread. Because he knew, without reading more, that the Alabama Supreme Court would refer only to the facts it liked, would use all the words in its arsenal to make the outcome seem reasonable and fair, even though it could never be reasonable or fair. When finally he gave in and read the rest of it, the numbness went away, to be replaced by anger.

The first sentences jolted him: "The Appellant was convicted of the offense of forcibly ravishing Elizabeth Liger, a white woman . . . the Appellant is of the negro race . . ."

Why mention their races like that, at the beginning of the opinion? It struck him as a taunt. There had been no claim that the trial was unfair due to racial prejudice. To be sure, he had thought about making such a claim when the only Negroes called for jury duty were struck, but he decided that word around town of such a pretrial motion would only inflame the Troy community, especially the white men who eventually would be the ones serving on the jury. Besides, the Scottsboro case didn't require Negroes on the jury, only that they be called for possible service. As for the trial itself, Judge Parks had run it tightly, keeping a firm hand on the spectators, holding a full squadron of the Highway Patrol at the ready.

The opinion continued: Charles White "allured" Elizabeth Liger to the home of Mary Etta Gray, "also of the negro race," where he "forcibly ravished her." There was nothing about the intact hymen, not one word about the absence of blood or bruises. The doctors who described Elizabeth Liger as having the mental development of a child were "competent" to give that opinion. The testimony about Elizabeth's obsession with fortune-tellers was permissible to show "the lure held out" by the defendant fortune-teller and his "accomplice," Mary Etta, "to inveigle the victim into the defendant's net." As for whether Judge Parks should have allowed him to ask, at the end of his cross-examination, "Miss Elizabeth, I will ask you again if this isn't a fact, that this negro was polite and courteous to you all the time that you were there?" the Supreme Court of Alabama held, "The question indicates on its face that it is a mere repetition," and calls for "a conclusion which it was the province of the jury to draw."

"THEY WANTED IT to come out this way, so they found ways to justify it," Bertha said, trying to console Foster. She had come straight to his office after teaching school, as the word spread around Enterprise of the Supreme Court's decision. "That's how the law works, isn't it? It works because even if we hate the result, we go along with it because it has been 'explained' to us, like we are children, and we don't know how to fight anymore."

He had no answer for that. "I don't know how to fight anymore," he said, drained of emotion. "And I feel as if I have been used. But I'm still writing the governor to ask for clemency. It probably won't do any good, but it's all I have left. The Supreme Court fixed his execution for June 9."

"I'll be in New York by then. Please call me or write something."

REGRETTABLY, I DON'T have a copy of any of the letters my mother wrote to my father about the New York World's Fair, but I know she wrote to him and I heard a lot about her visit.

Not surprisingly, Mother spent an entire afternoon not at the Fair but at the New York Public Library, believing she might never again have a chance to "feast on so many books." As for the Fair, she was not as interested in the Food Zone as in the Chrysler exhibit, where she watched a Plymouth being assembled in a theater with this new invention—specially cooled air, something we laughed about years later in Montgomery after the installation of our new window unit air conditioner. And there was a written account I so wish I could find—of how Mother, having eaten all the sandwiches and cookies she had packed in Alabama, finally treated herself to a meal in the big city—at an automat. My father, always one to avoid expensive places to eat, would have been keen for the fact that you could put a nickel in a slot and get a tasty pot pie, rice pudding, or chocolate cake. Indeed, years later, when we took a family trip in our green Nash automobile, once more eating sandwiches packed in Montgomery all the way to New York, our first meal "on the town" was at an automat.

I know my mother wrote in June 1939 to encourage my father, who was despondent after the decision by the Alabama Supreme Court, that there would someday be a brighter future. The motto of the New York World's Fair, she reminded him more than once, was "Dawn of a New Day."

ONE OF BERTHA'S June letters arrived in Enterprise on the morning of June 9, but Foster was not at his office to receive it, and when he returned late that afternoon, it was not the first thing he read. June 9 was the date set for the execution of Charles White, following the governor's denial of clemency, and the event was covered by the press. So the first thing he read was the newspaper.

Beneath the headline, "4 Die In Second Largest Mass Execution At Kilby," the *Montgomery Advertiser* reported that three of the negro convicts broke down, "admitting their crimes to L. C. Champney, negro chaplain." The article turned to the fourth man.

"Charles White, Alias, negro 'fortune teller' and conceded habitual criminal, came in to the death chamber confident and assured at 12:20. He protested that the electrode was fastened to his head too tightly, but attendants said his head was large and it was necessarily a 'tight fit.'"

Foster stopped, removed his glasses, and wiped his eyes. It made him sad to think of Charles having to put up with the final insult of a tight electrode, but he wanted to hug him for protesting the fit. The newspaper article continued:

"When asked, 'Do you realize you are about to die?' White quipped, 'Do I realize it!' and grinned. He then launched into a dramatic speech addressed to 'The Honorable Warden and to All Spectators.' He wound up with an assertion that he was 'Glad to go to Jesus an innocent man.' He was pronounced dead at 12:32 a.m."

Foster put the newspaper aside and sat at the rolltop desk his father had lent him and stared out his new window for a long time, until dusk, until the creamy white magnolia blossoms in front of the funeral home across the street were only faint outlines, pale, floating apparitions in the twilight. Then, getting up to leave the office, he noticed Bertha's unopened letter. It was getting dark in Enterprise, and Foster, with his poor eyesight, had to light the wick of his office lamp to make out what she wrote, about the wonders of the New York World's Fair and the Dawn of a New Day.

| Epilogue

OSTER DID ASK BERTHA if she would come back, and she returned to Enterprise from New York in the summer of 1939. After a long engagement—his idea—they married in 1941, in a civil ceremony with Frances as matron of honor. Both were surprised to learn, in 1942, that Bertha was pregnant, not something they had planned, given their precarious financial condition. The birth in early February of the following year was very difficult; Bertha came close to dying. (I remember her telling me that the Enterprise physician scolded her that she had no business becoming a mother at her age). The child, Joseph Madison, named for my father's double first cousin, Dr. Joseph Moxley, and, of course, for Mr. M. L., spent his first three weeks in the hospital nursery, happily watched over and entertained by female nurses and attendants, black and white, until Bertha was healthy enough to take him home.

THANKS TO A LETTER from my father to Mr. Yarbrough, his law partner, forwarded to me by an Enterprise lawyer, I know a little about his work in the years immediately after the Charles White case. With his law practice continuing to decline, he took a job with the War Department—the predecessor of the Department of Defense—as a closing attorney, and, later, as a project manager, for the Camp Rucker Military Project in Enterprise (today's Fort Rucker), examining titles to land, drafting conveyances, and disbursing purchase money. It was not work he talked about the way he talked about his trials, but at least it allowed him to remain in the town he loved. Then, even that was taken away. At an age, so I was told, when few men were drafted, and despite being blind in one eye, he was called in May 1943 to serve in the army by Coffee County authorities who had not forgotten or forgiven him for the Charles White case. He served initially as a private and was promoted to corporal before being honorably discharged when the war ended. He returned to Enterprise to find the remains of his meager practice securely in the hands of other lawyers. Unable to make a living as an attorney and at the same time help his father, who had closed his sawmill and M. L. Beck General Merchandise, and was on the verge of losing his remaining land, he moved his small family to Montgomery, where he took a job reviewing disability claims for the Veterans Administration. Yet he never stopped dreaming that he would someday return to Coffee County and again practice his beloved law. He even bought a vacant lot in Enterprise.

Foster Beck went to his death in 1973 believing that Charles White had not received justice.

As for my mother, she got a job teaching sixth grade in Montgomery, where she was highly sought after by parents and never forgotten by students. And while she always helped out by contributing part of her salary toward the family's needs, she always kept her own separate checking account.

IN THE FIRST YEARS of the new millennium, my family sponsored a series of lectures in honor of Foster Campbell Beck at Emory University. The inaugural speaker was the late Anthony Lewis, the author of *Gideon's Trumpet*, a Pulitzer Prize-winning book on the constitutional right to an attorney of indigent persons accused of serious crimes. Mr. Lewis was followed in succeeding years by Morris Dees, the founder of the Southern Poverty Law Center, a nonprofit organization in Montgomery, Alabama, devoted to fighting bigotry and hate; by Linda Greenhouse, the Supreme Court reporter for the *New York Times*; by Floyd Abrams, defender of the First Amendment, a professor at the Columbia University School of Journalism (and my worthy opponent in a case in which I represented the estate of Dr. Martin Luther King, Jr., and he represented CBS); and finally by the Honorable John Lewis, the civil rights hero. Congressman Lewis, who currently serves the district in Atlanta where I reside, was born in Troy, Alabama, in 1940, a year and a half after the trial of Charles White, Alias.

AND SO WE COME to the end of my father's story, but not to my curiosity about its possible connection with Harper Lee. In June 1992, I wrote to Eugene Winick, Harper Lee's New York literary agent at McIntosh and Otis. Gene and I had been on a fishing trip together in upstate New York, and when I told him about my father's case, he encouraged me to send a letter he could forward to Ms. Lee. Gene responded to me on July 6, forwarding a copy of Ms. Lee's letter to him, dated July 1, 1992.

I take Ms. Lee at her word—that she did not "recall" the case I described to her agent, that *To Kill a Mockingbird* was fiction. I don't doubt that her novel is fiction. But might stories about the Charles White case in Troy have filtered through to Monroeville, also in south Alabama, where Ms. Lee, at the time twelve years old, grew up? And might they somehow have inspired her novel, even though she had no conscious recollection of it sixty-six years later?

In her letter, Ms. Lee expressed skepticism that there would have been any newspaper publicity about my father's case, but having eventually obtained copies of multiple articles, I know for a fact that she was incorrect about that. Not only did the *Troy Messenger* report the arrest of Charles White in the front page article read by my father at the urging of Judge Parks; the *Alabama Journal*, in Montgomery, beneath the prominent all-caps headline "NEGRO ADMITS ATTACK IN TROY," wrote that a "six foot, 250 pound negro 'fortune teller' . . . first identified as C. W. White" confessed to attacking a Troy "white girl" and was sent to Kilby prison for his safety "when it became apparent feeling was getting pretty high" in Troy. The Troy and Montgomery newspapers ran other articles about the indictment, trial, sentencing, and execution, some of which I have cited or quoted from. I have heard that Ms. Lee's father was a south Alabama newspaper editor himself, as well as a lawyer; he might well have seen, read, and discussed some of the stories in the Montgomery and Troy papers. And in the South, at least in those days, there were the orally transmitted stories, especially likely to have been told and retold about something as unusual as a white Alabama lawyer vigorously defending a Negro man charged with rape of a white woman; about a trial in which the judge found it prudent to arrange for an armed escort of the Negro defendant back and forth between the courthouse and a distant prison, then to surround the courthouse throughout the trial with sixteen Highway Patrolmen in order to prevent a lynching. Such a trial likely would have been discussed in south Alabama—perhaps even in Ms. Lee's south Alabama hometown of Monroeville.

Besides the "obvious parallels," as Ms. Lee wrote, in the two stories, some of the details are similar. The trial of Charles White, a black man charged with raping a white woman, took place in 1938, in a small town in south Alabama; in the 1960 novel *Mockingbird*, the trial of a black man charged with raping a white woman was imagined to have occurred in 1935, just three years earlier, and also in a small town in south Alabama. In both cases there were threats to lynch the accused, prevented in my father's case by the well-publicized presence of the Alabama Highway Patrol, in *Mockingbird* when Scout shamed the mob outside the jail. And in *Mockingbird,* the alleged victim, Mayella Ewell, was a young woman of limited background and education, almost as much to be pitied as condemned, a woman in some ways much like Elizabeth "Cain" Liger.

Dr. Stewart's testimony that Elizabeth Liger was intact differs, of course, from what Harper Lee imagined in *Mockingbird*, where, to the apparent dismay of Atticus Finch, no doctor was even called to examine Mayella Ewell. Interestingly, however, in both the actual case and the fictional one, the alleged victim either did not manifest the physical traumas typical of rape—Elizabeth Liger was intact—or did not engage in intercourse with the defendant at all—Mayella Ewell's father interrupted her attempted seduction of Tom Robinson. Finally, the interactions between the accused men and the alleged victims strike me as an intriguing similarity. Atticus Finch told his jury that Mayella Ewell "did something that in our society is unspeakable: she kissed a black man." I think the jury must have believed Elizabeth Liger and Charles White did something unspeakable, even if there was no rape.

There are more trivial similarities. Both lawyers, known to be excellent shots, were nearly blind in one eye, both were men without wives (Atticus was a widower), both were ahead of their times on the subject of race, and both represented poor families, sometimes being paid in produce, which was all that many of their clients could afford during those Depression years.

But there are differences as well: the man Harper Lee imagined as Atticus in *Mockingbird* was a seasoned attorney "of nearly fifty," while my father was a much younger man. In the aftermath of the fictional case, Bob Ewell's eventual attack on Jem was a personal vendetta, after which Atticus Finch resumed his professional life, whereas my father ultimately lost his law practice.

I have great admiration for Ms. Lee and *To Kill a Mockingbird*—such a classic that a few years ago, the *New York Times* reported it was still selling some 750,000 copies annually, and that was well before *Go Set a Watchman*. That same article also reported that Ms. Lee had stopped talking to the press in 1965, and for years, I heard her described as "reclusive." Still, this reclusive lady notified my client, the publishers Houghton Mifflin, of her support of a widely publicized case I was defending—the alleged copyright infringement of the book and movie *Gone with the Wind* by a parody, *The Wind Done Gone*. This was a surprising move by Ms. Lee—and one much appreciated by me—and I sometimes wonder if my earlier correspondence with her agent played any role in her decision to step forward in such a public way. More likely, she was just sympathetic to my clients, the publisher and the African American author, Alice Randall, and willing to go on the record in their defense.

So I will leave it at this: as men of courage and conviction, the Atticus Finch of *Mockingbird* and my father were birds of a feather. Alabamians should take pride not only in native daughter Harper Lee, creator of the fictional lawyer who inspired so many, but also in native son Foster Campbell Beck, a real Alabama lawyer.

Appendix

I N AN EFFORT to maintain the pace of the foregoing narrative, I have deferred explaining how I came to discover the facts of the Charles White case. Although I had heard about the case, by the time I began to take a real interest in it, my father was dead. That was when I belatedly realized that I didn't even know the name of his client.

My search began in earnest when I hired someone in Montgomery—I lived in Atlanta by then, and it was before digitization of many public records—to review any mentions of my father or his law firm in cases before the Alabama Supreme Court in the 1930s. I had remembered my father telling me he appealed the case to the Alabama Supreme Court.

An initial discovery was of a case appealing the conviction of an alleged murderer, but a review of the second case, *State of Alabama v. Charles White, Alias,* involving an alleged rape by a black man of a white woman in Troy, Alabama, coupled with the mention of my father's law firm as counsel, left no doubt that this was the one. Now that I had the name of the case and of my father's client, I was able

to obtain, for a modest fee, the search results from the very helpful Alabama Department of Archives and History. The Troy and
Montgomery newspapers published a number of articles about the
case, which apparently had caused quite a stir in south Alabama, and
the Alabama Department of Archives and History had copies of at
least some of those articles. (Interestingly to me, the papers carried
slightly varied accounts of some of the facts, perhaps because of the
need to rely on reports from citizens in the field and to meet press
deadlines; for example, in addition to the slight differences in the
arrest and indictment dates reported by the *Troy Messenger* and the
Montgomery Advertiser, noted above in the narrative, the *Alabama
Journal* described the victim as "a 16 year old" and wrote that "the
negro robbed and attacked her after enticing her into a house on
the pretext of 'telling her fortune.'" Elizabeth Liger testified at trial
under oath that she was twenty, and there is no mention of her having been robbed.)

Once again, the Alabama Department of Archives and History,
namely Dr. Norwood Kerr, was helpful in tracking documentary
items of interest. Dr. Kerr confirmed that he had sent me everything
in the Archives about the case, and also confirmed my memory of
Hank Aaron's performance for Jacksonville before being called up
to the Milwaukee Braves.

Importantly, I obtained from Dr. Kerr a copy of the trial transcript, which included not only the names of the judge, solicitor,
alleged victim, and witnesses, but also the witnesses' testimony and
the charges by the judge to the jury. I remember the chill that went
up my spine when I recognized my father's handwritten notations
and signature on the transcript.

I was less successful in obtaining information about the other principals. I found no mention of the trial judge, William L. Parks, the alleged victim, Elizabeth Liger, or of the Charles White case in the history of Pike County that I purchased from the Troy library. The two references to Solicitor Ewell C. Orme, who prosecuted Charles White, refer to him only as a "Troy attorney" who became president of a fertilizer company in 1952. In a response to my letter of inquiry, a Troy attorney who practiced law with E. C. Orme "for approximately 20 years" wrote that he had no information about the Charles White case, noting that it had been tried and appealed six years before his birth. Correspondence and conversations with others in Troy produced no new information, although I was eventually able to obtain a copy of the jury summons list thanks to a Troy State University professor.

By purchasing a copy of the death certificate, I learned that Elizabeth "Cain" Liger died in a Montgomery hospital on October 28, 1964. The "main cause of death was pulmonary edema caused by ovarian cancer." Apparently, she never married. A search turned up no heirs, no surviving brothers or sisters, and no reference to her part in the case.

Nor could I find any information about the Charles White case through those who knew my father's law partner, a much older man I only heard referred to as Mr. Yarbrough, in particular what role, if any, he had played in the case. My father's handwritten family history records that after the Troy lawyers "managed to get employed as special prosecutor or used other excuses" to avoid being appointed to defend Charles White, the judge "on a personal basis" asked "my partner and me to defend the case." Yet other than that sentence (and a mention in the *Messenger* that the day after the trial, Mr. Yarbrough announced they would appeal), I know of no active part he took in the trial.

The two-person law firm Yarbrough and Beck is listed as counsel, but that was the practice then (and often now) when an attorney in a law firm takes a case. I read the reference to "my partner and me" as my father's expression of pride in his law firm, in his new partnership at the firm, rather than as an acknowledgment of any subsequent participation in the case by Mr. Yarbrough. I know from his family history and our conversations that he had tried cases alone prior to the Charles White case.

Mr. Yarbrough was described in an article (publisher unknown), forwarded to me by an Enterprise lawyer who knew him, as a "most civic minded" man who "pushed for the paving of the streets" in Enterprise and who was the first president of the Enterprise Chamber of Commerce and a charter member of the Enterprise Rotary Club; however, there was no mention in the article of any of his accomplishments as a lawyer—which is consistent with my mother's comment to me that Mr. Yarbrough was "more interested in business than in law." Even his obituary, other than referring to him as a "prominent Enterprise attorney" who served as city attorney for several years, mentions no clients or cases, but instead reports that he was "a charter member of the Enterprise Rotary Club, Shriner, Deacon in the First Baptist Church, first president of the Chamber of Commerce, served several terms as Commander of American Legion Post . . . He played a major part in securing Fort Rucker for this area during World War II."

As for the mention in the *Messenger* that after the trial Mr. Yarbrough announced there would be an appeal, it is possible, given other conflicting press details about the case, that the reporter read the defense firm name Yarbrough and Beck and merely cited the first name in the firm. But it is also possible (though I never heard this) that Mr. Yarbrough actually came, if not to the trial, then the following day to the sentencing, and—perhaps influenced by his young partner's passion and determination—said there would be an appeal. On the other hand, even though I don't think he played any significant role in the case, the fact that he did not terminate the partnership as a result of my father's agreement to represent Charles White speaks well of him.

Finally, as noted in the text, neither of the Enterprise lawyers who remembered the firm of Yarbrough and Beck knew anything about the Charles White case or believed that any of the files would have been retained. And inquiries I published in the *Enterprise Ledger*, a paid circulation daily, and in the local free paper, asking if anyone remembered my father or his law firm, produced no responses.

So that is the combination of plenitude and dearth in which I composed.

THE BECK AND STEWART family names—even the name Abraham Lincoln Stewart, an unusual name, to say the least, for an Alabama boy in the early 1900s—are all the real names of those family members. My mother's father really did send the socialist Eugene Debs, being held in the Atlanta Federal Penitentiary, a pillow. Foster, Bertha, and Mr. M. L.—whose pictures are included in this appendix—are as true to their characters as I could make them. The newspaper articles mentioned are all from the Alabama Archives and are quoted or summarized accurately. The quotations from the Alabama Supreme Court are verbatim, from the opinion in the case; and the report of the testimony in the trial of Charles White comes directly from the transcript, also verbatim except for the redaction of some redundancies and the rephrasing or summarizations of some evidentiary objections in the interest of clarity and brevity.

A photocopy of the handwritten letter from Dr. George Washington Carver to Mr. M. L., and one of the letter about the other charges against Charles White, are also included here, as is a photograph of the Pike County Courthouse, courtesy of the Troy City Library, as it existed around the time of the trial.

I hope you have enjoyed joining my father and mother on their adventure at least half as much as I have enjoyed spending time in their company again.

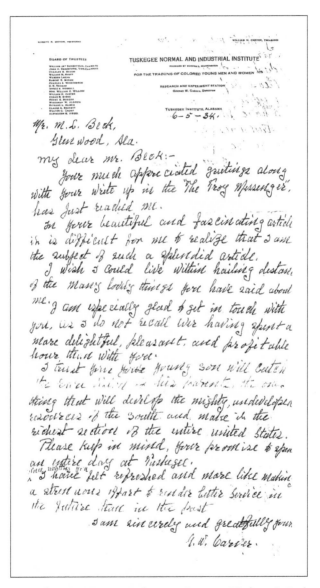

Letter from Dr. George Washington Carver to Madison L. Beck
(courtesy of Tuskegee University)

STATE OF ALABAMA
BOARD OF ADMINISTRATION
PRISON AT

Montgomery, Ala.
June 16, 1938.

Mr. Burr R. Reeves,
Sheriff, Pike County,
Troy, Ala.

Dear Sir:

Herewith is criminal record of James White, our #S-91 negro male, being held at Kilby Prison on safe keeping charge for your office.

As, Charles White #11113, received at State Prison, Jackson, Mich., Jan. 25, 1917 under sentence of 5 to 10 years for Armed Robbery.

As, Charles White #52678, received at State Prison, Columbus, Ohio, Jan. 17, 1924 under sentence of 20 to 30 years for Burglary of Inhabited Dwelling.

As, Charles White #1376, arrested by Police, Springfield, Ohio, Nov. 14, 1934, charge Rape, no disposition of charge given.

As, C.W.White #8145, arrested by Police, Seattle, Wash., 7-8-1919, charge Robbery, no disposition of charge given, other than he was turned over to the Sheriff there, 7-11-1919.

As, Herbert Wm. White #181, arrested by Sheriff, Panama City, Florida, 3-29-1937, charge Investigation, no disposition of charge given.

With every best wish, I am

Yours very truly,

H.B.Brown, Supt.,
State Bureau of Criminal Identification,
Kilby Prison.

HBB/b-

Charles White's prior arrests (courtesy of Pike County Courthouse)

Foster C. Beck

Madison L. Beck (Mr. M. L.)

Bertha Stewart

Two views of Pike County Courthouse (courtesy of the Holman Johnson Collection, Troy Public Library)

| Acknowledgments

FIRST AND FOREMOST, I thank my wife and daughters for their interest, encouragement, guidance, criticisms, and unflagging support. There were times when I only persevered with this endeavor in order that my children might have a record of their paternal grandfather and great-grandfather, both of whom were dead before their births. (Happily, they knew my mother, who lived long enough to meet and love my daughters and to bring them tins of homemade chocolate chip cookies from Montgomery. I owe my family more than I can ever repay.)

I gratefully acknowledge my debt to my friend and terrific literary agent, Wendy Strothman, who patiently and professionally read and commented on an earlier draft, guided me to the right publisher, and supported me throughout the process of editing and eventual publication. I also want to thank Wendy's associate, Lauren Macleod, for her able assistance throughout.

Starling (Star) Lawrence at W. W. Norton, a legendary editor with whom I am honored to work, acquired the manuscript, gave it a careful reading that improved it substantially—not least by restraining my litigation lawyer's propensity to overuse italics—and, with others at Norton, came up with the title. Star's assistant, Ryan Harrington, provided expert help in tracking edits and in the many unfamiliar (for this previously unpublished book author) ins and outs of publishing. Thanks also to Kathleen Carter Zrelak, Allegra Huston, Elizabeth Riley, Louise Mattarelliano, and Anna Mageras.

Some or all of a draft of the manuscript was read or commented on by my friends (in alphabetical order) Nancy Abrams, Elaine Alexander, Miles Alexander, Esq., Ellen Emerson, Nancy Grote, Jane Hawkins (besides being a friend, Jane is my cousin and the younger daughter of my father's sister, the wonderful and beloved Frances), Dr. Mel Konner, Dr. Ann Kruger, Dr. Maryann McGuire, Dr. Peter Mcguire, Sam Rosen, Esq., Noel L. Silverman, Esq., Dr. John Sitter, Michael W. Tyler, Esq., and Arthur York, Esq. I am indebted and sincerely grateful to each of them for their time and encouragement. Special additional thanks to Kate Ravin, a professional technical editor, for offering helpful suggestions throughout the draft, and to Troy Hendrick, Esq., an expert criminal defense lawyer, for assisting this civil litigator with questions about criminal procedure.

Dr. Norwood Kerr of the Alabama Department of Archives and History was—as noted in the appendix—very helpful in locating the transcript and newspaper articles, confirming I had everything pertaining to the case, and in verifying my memory of such details as Hank Aaron's first game against the Montgomery Rebels.

Special thanks also to Donna Rizzo, who was willing, after hours from her regular job, to help me with research and typing; to Karen Bullard at the Troy City Library, for the photographs of the courthouse that are included and for suggesting that I purchase the Troy and Pike County history mentioned in the narrative; and to

Jo Ann Messick, at the Pike County Clerk's Office, who forwarded me a copy of the record of prior convictions of Charles White, alias C. W. White, alias Herbert Wm. White, and who confirmed that I had a copy of everything in the courthouse file (I had visited the courthouse earlier and conducted my own search).

Thanks to Joe Cassady, Sr., a prominent Enterprise lawyer who practiced for a while with Mr. Yarbrough after my father left the firm. Mr. Cassady (whose distinguished father was a friend of Mr. M. L. in Glenwood) kindly spoke with me to confirm that Mr. Yarbrough's son, daughters, and other family members had all passed away, making it impossible for me to talk to any of them, and also to confirm that he had no knowledge of *State of Alabama v. Charles White, Alias* and that the files on cases from the 1930s had not been retained by the firm. Thanks also to Mr. Cassady's respected former law partner and friend, Dale Marsh, a distinguished Enterprise attorney with an interest in history and the law profession, for forwarding a 1948 letter from my father to Mr. Yarbrough, thanking him for visiting him in Montgomery and asking for a description of his work in Enterprise as a lawyer and reference to support a job application to the Veterans Administration. Thanks also to prominent Troy attorney Joseph Faulk, who wrote that although he practiced law with E. C. Orme, he had no information about *State of Alabama v. Charles White, Alias*, noting that the case was appealed six years prior to Mr. Faulk's birth. He did not think that Mr. Orme's daughter would know anything about the case.

Finally, thanks to my high school classmate Dr. James Vickery, for putting me in touch with his Troy State University colleague Ed Stevens. Ed helpfully found and sent me a copy of the list of potential jurors and spoke with his Troy lawyer friends, who confirmed that all the lawyers and judges practicing at the time were deceased and that there was nothing else in the court files.

Permissions to reproduce the Carver letter, the lines from Congressman Lewis's book, and the excerpts from the Troy and Montgomery papers were all graciously granted.